War can bring out the best as well as the worst in people. Some achieve the heights of leadership; others assume the role of commanders leading men into battle; still others are destined to be led.

The word *great* has been applied by historians to many military figures since the close of World War II. At the top of any such list you will inevitably find many Germans. Through training and ability, the German military system produced some of the world's most highly qualified commanders. Their excellence in the battlefield brought most of Europe and North Africa under German domination.

Guderian, Rommel, von Manstein, Kesselring, Von Rundstedt, Hausser: Though their cause may now be in question, they will go down in history as some of

THE GREAT COMMANDERS OF WORLD WAR II

THE GREAT COMMANDERS OF WORLD WAR II

Volume I: THE GERMANS

BY CHARLES E. PFANNES AND VICTOR A. SALAMONE

ZEBRA BOOKS

KENSINGTON PUBLISHING CORP.

ZEBRA BOOKS

are published by

KENSINGTON PUBLISHING CORP.
21 East 40th Street
New York, N.Y. 10016

Second printing: August 1985

TABLE OF CONTENTS

FOR POP:
ONLY A VOLUNTEER
BUT THE GREATEST CHIEF OF ALL

Preface

War brings out the best and occasionally the worst in people. Some achieve the heights of leadership, others assume the role of commanders leading men into battle, while still others are destined to be led.

The word great has been applied by historians to many military figures since the close of World War II. On the top of the list you would inevitably find many German commanders.

Through training and ability, the German military system produced some of the most qualified commanders whose excellence on the battlefield brought most of Europe and North Africa under German domination.

We have elected to portray the following six German commanders whom we feel exemplify the qualities of a commander. We have tried to present for each commander a brief biography emphasizing his background, training, and influences. For the six selected commanders, however, we will stress one or more campaigns which we feel he conducted with brilliance and élan.

Colonel General Heinz Guderian, though known as the Father of the Blitzkrieg, will be shown for his dash and zeal that led to the breakout at Sedan and rapid movement to the channel coast which brought France to its knees in a mere six weeks.

For experience in command we turn next to Germany's most senior officer, Field Marshal Gerd von Rundstedt. Hitler relied on the experience of this commander throughout the war. In Poland, France, Russia, and Western Europe, the Fuhrer turned to this stabilizing influence.

For our next selection we turn to perhaps the most popularized German Commander, Field Marshal Erwin Rommel. Though his career is dotted by brilliance, it is by virtue of his Gazala campaign of May/June 1942, resulting in the fall of Tobruk that we see portrayed all his talents: his strategical ability, his craftiness which earned him the nickname of the 'desert fox', his style of command of leading from the front, and his ability to do the unexpected.

Next we come to Field Marshal Erich von Manstein, Germany's brilliant tactician who designed the plan which brought France to its knees in six weeks. It is, however, by virtue of his miraculous conduct during and after the fall of Stalingrad in which he saved the German Army from total disaster, giving them one more chance of destroying the Russians in 1943, that we have chosen him.

Now we portray Field Marshal Albert Kesselring, 'smiling Albert' as the Allies called him. We see in Kesselring a man who against all opposition risked his reputation and conducted a magnificent prolonged defense in Italy which tied down a large Allied force for the duration of the war.

Lastly we come to SS General Paul Hausser. Though an arm of the Nazi State, the Waffen SS did manage to produce some highly qualified commanders, Paul Hausser being one of them. His wise actions and brilliant moves at Kharkov in 1943 which staved off defeat and momentarily brought a victory for the Germans and his brilliant extradition of the forces at Falaise in France earn him a place as one of Germany's great commanders.

Though we have limited ourselves to six commanders, this does not exclude the many other excellent commanders produced by Germany during the Second World War. These six, however, will give the reader a fine representation of the 'type' of commander produced in Germany. From them we can learn about the many other brilliant military leaders spawned by the Germans.

In closing we would like to thank the many people who have helped us in the production of this book. We particularly want to thank Peter Brent for introducing the authors to each other.

C. Pfannes

V. Salamone

November, 1980

Poughkeepsie, New York

Introduction

Excellent, brilliant, and efficient are but a few of the superlatives used to describe the Great German General Staff. In a sense, the General Staff bred military greatness so that each generation could share the lessons of the past in pursuit of military prowess.

Throughout this book, the reader will find references to the German General Staff. Through the years the General Staff in Germany had exerted a dramatic influence on the extent of Germany's military greatness. The authors feel that a short introduction of the history and the nature of the German General Staff will help the reader understand the background of the six commanders examined in this volume.

The origins of the German Army General Staff go back to the early days of Prussia. Though the term General Staff was frequently used, in reality it did not refer to a particular group of specially trained staff officers. Instead, in time of war, a staff would be assembled that would have responsibility for the conduct of that specific conflict.

The true beginnings of the German General Staff traces its roots to the reforms that were introduced in Prussia after its disasterous humiliation by Napoleon at Jena in 1806. In the midst of defeat, Gerhard Scharnhorst, recognizing the need for military reform, organized what we now know as the German General Staff. Scharnhorst's great desire was to bring the army and the nation into a more intimate union. The army in Prussia thus came to be regarded as a pillar of the state in the same way as the family and the schools.

In 1810, the War College was established in Berlin to provide selected officers with the knowledge of tactics, strategy, military technology, map reading, geography, languages, and administration, required for higher command. The best, most qualified students would then be appointed to the General Staff. Entrance to the War College was based on passage of a competitive exam. After passing the exam, the aspirant would then enter the college. At graduation, the young officer would find himself assigned to the Great General Staff for two years further experience in topographical study, map exercises, and war games. Only then was the staff officer allowed to don the distinctive red trouser stripes of the General Staff. Officers who had successfully completed the War College and General Staff Training habitually were given better assignments and more rapid promotion.

Thus, the establishment of the War College was a major step in insuring a permanent supply of highly specialized professionals. From this small group of carefully selected officers, there developed, during and after the wars of liberation against Napoleon, a specially constructed, permanent general staff system with a central authority known as the Great General Staff that exercised its control through those staff officers who filled positions at corps and divisional headquarters.

As the army increased in size, so too did the need for a trained body of General Staff officers. The need for well trained specialists was essentially to keep the army informed and properly commanded.

"A General Staff is a highly trained, carefully selected group of military generalists whose function in peace or war is to assist the nation's military leadership."[1]

With the permanent establishment of the General Staff system, Prussia, and later Germany, guaranteed that their army would be served by a well trained, highly disciplined group of professionals. As Clausewitz, a former Chief of the General Staff put it, "Since the state could not exist undefended, the survival of the Army had priority over that of the state". The General Staff thus became a major organ of the nation.

There were many significant features of the Prussian staff system that later came to typify its mode of operation. First, the General Staff was semi-autonomous within the confines of the much larger War Ministry. Secondly, its officers were trained in military doctrine and theory. Finally, General Staff officers were rotated between the Great General Staff and positions with formations in the field.

The great victories of the German Army under von Moltke during the chancellorship of Otto von Bismark portrayed to the world the quality of German military excellence.

In the Twentieth Century the General Staff faced its most demanding test during the First World War. Though Germany was defeated, the military had beaten Russia and made an Allied victory extremely difficult. It did in fact, blame Germany's collapse not on itself, but on the politicians who 'stabbed Germany in the back'. Thus, the proud tradition of the German General Staff managed to survive amid the humiliation of defeat.

The General Staff and the War College were both outlawed by the harsh terms of the Treaty of Versailles. Thanks, however, to the machinations of General Hans van Seeckt, both institutions survived, although disguised, until 1935 when their original name was resumed. Von Seeckt sought to make the 100,000 man army allowed by Versailles, an army of leaders; an elite force. He saw as one of his most important tasks, the preservation of the spirit of the original General Staff. Among the 4,000 officers allowed the Reichswehr, a large proportion were members of the old General Staff. Though the War College was prohibited, von Seeckt saw to it that each military district was responsible for conducting General Staff training. He also placed heavy emphasis on the non-political nature of the army and raised that theory to almost a religious doctrine. This policy would come to exert a strong influence on a number of highly placed military leaders during World War II.

After Hitler's ascent to power and his subsequent overthrow of the restraints of Versailles, the Great General Staff came out of hiding.

The attitude of the General Staff Officers towards the new master of Germany was one of ambivalence. They were torn between the prospect of a greater Germany versus the vulgarity and crudeness of the Nazis. Throughout the short life of the Third Reich, the General Staff was torn between human, ethical and patriotic duty on one side and military obedience as exemplified in their military oath on the other. This continual conflict eventually led to the final destruction of the General Staff climaxing in an attempt by a number of staff officers to assassinate Hitler. Following the failure of this attempted coup, Hitler resolved to destroy the General Staff.

The long history of German military greatness ended in the shambles of the destruction of the Third Reich. The campaigns conducted so expertly by the General Staff were squandered by the mad policies of a crazed dictator.

Contrary to popular belief, not all General officers were qualifed General Staff members. Of the Generals whose careers are examined here, Von Rundstedt, von Manstein, Guderian and Kesselring were General Staff members. Incredible as it may seem, Germany's most renowned General, Rommel, never earned the right to wear the General Staff uniform. On the other hand, SS General Paul Hausser had been a qualifed General Staff officer who tired of the constant boredom of staff duty, retired, and rejoined the military as a member of the Waffen SS.

At the Nuremberg trials in 1946, the tribunal which condemned General Alfred Jodl and Hitler's lackey, Field Marshal Wilhelm Keitel to death for specific crimes against humanity, also ruled that the General Staff could not be convicted as a criminal organization and all criminal charges against its members were dropped.

The Great General Staff passed into history but it went with its reputation intact. Today, when one reflects upon the Germany of the last two centuries, the Great General Staff will loom large in that reflection.

Chapter 1

Probably no single individual exerted as dramatic an influence on the tactical conduct of World War II as Colonel General Heinz Guderian, father of the Panzer Division and creator of the Blitzkrieg. Technically, Guderian was not the inventor of the latter—he simply took hold of other people's ideas and molded them into a precise tactical formula. In his hands, it provided Germany with an instrument of terror and destruction that allowed her to run up an incredible string of swift, devastating victories which saw virtually all of Europe, with few exceptions, succumb to the might of the Nazi colossus.

Of all the prominent German Generals of World War II, only Rommel was to attain greater notoriety. Serious students of the war, military historians, and professional soldiers attribute Guderian's fame to the revolutionary contributions made towards the art of warfare. By his advocacy of the use of tanks in an independent role, Guderian paved the path to his immortality.

Heinz Guderian was born in June of 1888 in East Prussia. His father was in the military which could not but help form the milieu into which young Heinz was raised. In German History, Guderian's birth coincided with the ascension of Kaiser Wilhelm II to the throne of Germany.

At the age of thirteen, young Heinz entered cadet school where he studied until he was sixteen, at which time he entered principle cadet school, his brother Fritz following shortly thereafter.

In January 1908, Guderian received his Lieutenant's commission and was promptly posted to an infantry battalion commanded by the young officer's father.

With energy that was to typify Guderian's later career, the youthful Lieutenant plunged himself fully into the pursuit of his lifelong career. After a series of routine junior assignments with the infantry, he was selected in 1912 to join one of the newly created radio companies. (Radio as a military asset was then in its infancy). During this brief assignment, Guderian came to appreciate the various methods by which radio might improve combat efficiency, particularly for the control of swift moving formations.

In early 1913, at the age of twenty-five, he became the youngest officer selected to attend the war academy. Erich von Manstein was attending at the same time. By October of the same year, feeling secure in his profession, he married Margarete Goerne.

August of 1914 saw Europe cataclysmically plunged into a war from which she would never recover. Every nation was armed to the teeth and carrying ancient grudges that they were anxious to avenge. Guderian found himself assigned to a heavy wireless station attached to a cavalry corps. His prior experience in radio communications fitted him well for this assignment. Although not in the front line, he did participate in the battles of Ypres and in Flanders on the Western front before his transfer to the intelligence branch in January of 1916. In February, 1918, Guderian received the coveted appointment to membership in the General Staff Corps. Ironically, the man who was to provide the greatest contribution to the development of the tank in an independent role and who was to champion the cause of directing operations from the front, himself missed most of the significant tank battles of World War I while serving at headquarters and in other rear area assignments.

After World War I, his talent and dedication earned him selection as one of the relative handful of officers allotted to Germany's small army by the harsh terms of the Treaty of Versailles.

In 1922, Guderian was appointed to the Inspectorate of Transport Troops whose object was to develop motorized transport for use in battle. At this time, in order to supplement his salary, he started writing for military journals and began to look at the tank, considering possible alternative uses for the machine in future operations.

Throughout the decade of the 20s, Guderian concentrated on improving tank performance, developing theories, and studying the teachings of Fuller, Liddel-Hart, and Martel. In PANZER LEADER, Guderian states:

"It was principally the books and articles of the Englishmen, Fuller, Liddel-Hart, and Martel that excited my interest and gave me food for thought. These far sighted soldiers were even then trying to make of the tank something more than just an infantry support weapon. They envisioned it in relationship to the growing motorization of our age, and thus they became the pioneers of a new type of warfare on the largest scale."[1]

Because few German officers took the role of the tank seriously, Guderian soon became the resident authority on the use of tanks in battle.

In 1931, General Lutz became Inspector General of Motorized Troops and Guderian was selected as his Chief of Staff. Lutz was a forward thinking officer and one of the most liberal in the German Army at that time. Therefore, Guderian, who had previously served with Lutz, was given a relatively free hand to develop and practice his theories.

By 1933, the first foundations of the Panzer Divisions were being laid by Guderian under the watchful and protective eye of Lutz. Unfortunately, the Chief of the General Staff, General Ludwig Beck, saw little merit in Guderian's revolutionary ideas and did little to encourage development of the tank. Instead, Beck, through the use of his office, attempted to thwart armoured development. It has been suggested that Beck's attitude stemmed from his desire to deny Hitler the use of a potentially victorious weapon.

However, anyone familiar with Beck's career would readily agree that he was a traditionalist, and as such, was incapable of looking favorably upon unique ideas that were contrary to the established methods. Although a brilliant staff officer and a decent man who was to meet a tragic end*, he was appalled when Guderian proposed that an armoured commander lead his formation from the front while maintaining contact with headquarters via radio. Guderian was bluntly informed that a commander's proper place was at his headquarters during battle.

In spite of Beck's passive resistance, 1934 saw the creation of the first infant Panzer Division with tanks being assigned to motorized divisions. Guderian now set about training this unit in the use of his tactics. However, it wasn't until a favorable impression was made on Hitler during maneuvers that further creation of an armoured force was allowed to proceed in earnest. In 1935, three Panzer Divisions were formed with Guderian given command of one of them.

In 1936, ACHTUNG PANZER, penned by Guderian was published. The book expounded the theory of massed armoured formations working closely with air units to be used rather as flying artillery. First must be the breakthrough on a narrow front, the Schwerpunkt. The tanks, being concentrated in mass, would then head quickly for the enemy's main defensive zone

* Beck was one of the leaders of the conspiracy against Hitler. With the failure of the assassination attempt on July 20, 1944, he was allowed to take his own life.

before the latter's guns could have any effect on the battle. Once the breakthrough was achieved, closely knit teams of infantry would mop up the gun areas and fixed defenses. Guderian emphasized that the initial expansion must be on a relatively narrow front. The one fatal error would be to pause and give the enemy time to regain his balance and locate and concentrate against the attacker, for as long as the panzers retained their mobility and continued on the move, the enemy would find himself unable to regain his balance. This publication, with its theories, served to thaw the German preference for a fixed defense. That year also saw Guderian's promotion to Major General.

During the turbulent days following the Blomberg-Fritsch crisis*, many generals were removed from their commands, including Guderian's mentor, Lutz, who was sent into retirement. Guderian succeeded him as commander of mobile troops. He, in his typical forthright manner, sought Hitler's cooperation in expanding the Panzer forces. The German dictator readily pledged his personal support for Guderian's plans.

By the end of 1938, there existed five full Panzer Divisions, another in the process of forming, and four Light Divisions whose motorized capability allowed for rapid upgrading to full Panzer Division status should the need occur. What Guderian now needed was a practical demonstration of the capability of these units.

Unfortunately, the Panzers failed miserably

* When Generals Blomberg and Fritsch, War Minister and C. In C. of the Army respectively, began to resist Hitler's path towards war, they were disgraced on trumped up charges and relieved of their commands.

during the German march into Austria in March of 1938. However, many important lessons were learned, foremost of which was the need to pay greater attention to the logistical support of the Panzer Divisions. This was painfully obvious as tanks ran out of fuel, frequently broke down and were caught in traffic jams during the Anchluss. Guderian was in an excellent position to witness this, having commanded the XVI Corps. By the time Hitler marched into Poland in September of 1938, most of the logistical and support problems had been ironed out by Guderian and his staff. Poland would make the world sit up and take notice.

On August 22, 1939, Guderian received orders to command the XIX Corps consisting of the 2nd and 20th Motorized Divisions and the 3rd Panzer Division commanded by General Leo Geyr von Schweppenberg. XIX Corps was to spearhead the attack of General Fedor von Bock's assault on the Polish corridor.

With negotiations rapidly breaking down, Hitler targeted September 1, as the day to unleash his blitzkrieg against the powerless Poles. The Nazi-Soviet Pact which Germany signed with Russia on August 23, 1939 allowed Hitler to secure his Eastern border; thus hopefully averting the possibility of Soviet interference and the creation of a two front war. On the designated morning, the blitzkreig was unleashed in its full fury, causing horrible devastation to the outgunned and outnumbered Polish Army which was quickly routed or destroyed where it stood.

Striking through the Polish corridor, Guderian travelled in his command car with the leading elements of the 3rd Panzer Division. On the first day, the leading units of XIX Corps approached the Guderian ancestral home at Gross Klovia in former German territory which had been surrendered at Versailles in order to create the infamous corridor. Finding the 3rd Panzer Division halted, he personally intervened and managed to get the division moving once more. After a mere five days, Polish resistance in the corridor was shattered and ceased to exist.

Now Guderian ordered his corps on a wide flanking drive to the West of Warsaw. Rapidly cutting off two Polish armies, his units advanced down the West bank of the River Bug and on September 17, made contact with the units of General Erich Hoeppner's XVI Panzer Corps advancing from the South. Thus was formed an iron ring around the Polish Army. Meanwhile, General Gerd von Rundstedt's Army Group South, advancing from Silesia, smashed the remaining Poles against the outer edges of the circle drawn by Guderian and Hoeppner.

Vindication for Guderian was complete. Beyond a shadow of a doubt, he had proven that Panzers could indeed operate independently and force a decisive conclusion to a battle.

After the battle of the corridor, Hitler toured the battlefield. Awed at the carnage and wreckage of the Polish artillery, he asked whether the Luftwaffe's Stukas had created such enormous damage. Guderian promptly answered, "No, it was our Panzers!" Hitler was sold. The tour made a lasting impression on the commander of Hitler's bodyguard who was accompanying the Fuhrer on the tour. This young Colonel would himself utilize this doctrine and achieve lasting fame. His name? Erwin Rommel.

Thus, while Austria provided the opportunity for the Panzers to recognize their logistical shortcomings and iron them out, Poland afforded the chance to hone their tactics of Blitzkrieg to a fine edge which during the next few years would prove to be unstoppable.

During the period of lull on the Western Front, dubbed the "Phoney War", another German General, Erich von Manstein was looking with skepticism upon the accepted German plan for the invasion of France. After taking heed of his reservations, von Manstein devised an alternative. (See Manstein, Chapter 4). The new plan called for a shifting of the German schwerpunct from von Bock's Army Group opposite the Lowlands, to von Rundstedt's striking out of the Ardennes Forest. Manstein realized that for his plan to be successful, it required the complete support of the Panzer arm and the ability of the tank to traverse the difficult terrain of the heavily wooded Ardennes. Consequently, before he could seriously submit his plan of attack, he sought the advice of a tank expert and thus Guderian found himself an integral part of the Manstein Plan.

After an extensive study of the terrain,

Guderian was able to assure Manstein that the Panzers could indeed handle the difficult assignment but he insisted that that the attack would be successful only if two conditions were met. First, the Panzers must be accompanied by motorized infantry who would secure the void created by the wake of the rapidly advancing spearhead until such time as regular infantry divisions became available to occupy these positions. Secondly, the Panzers should be concentrated in formations powerful enough to force their way through the French strongholds. General Halder* had proposed the use of a weaker concentration of armour but this Guderian forcefully opposed with his second condition.

Although the overall concept was Manstein's, it was Guderian who selected the focal point for the attack over the Meuse River at Sedan. Once across, Guderian proposed exploiting the breakthrough with a rapid advance towards Amiens and the French coast. Once again, Halder expressed his disagreement. The latter's conservative approach called for the Panzers to wait at Sedan for the following infantry to catch up before resuming the attack westward. Guderian's argument that this concept would sacrifice the essential element of surprise, won the day.

Forseeing these problems of having the plan accepted, Guderian commissioned a

* General Franz Halder, Chief of the German General Staff.

thorough survey of the French fortifications in the area by his engineering officer. Basing his conclusions on the results of this survey, he insisted upon an all out attack in force to be unleashed immediately with little attention given to flank protection. In this he found himself in complete accord with General von Wietersham, slated to command the motorized infantry that was to follow behind the armoured advance.

Although unable to offer concrete evidence as to the feasibility of the campaign, Guderian concluded that the French leadership had little stomach for the forthcoming struggle. Though he respected the French fighting man, he was convinced that the French possessed few reserves with which to threaten his exposed and vulnerable flanks should the breakthrough prove successful.

In February of 1940, a series of war games were conducted at General Sigmund List's Twelfth Army Headquarters with the Meuse crossing the primary focus of study. There was an enormous amount of disbelief in the Manstein/Guderian plan. General List desired the infantry divisions to lead across the Meuse; Rundstedt wavered and demonstrated a lack of tank appreciation by declining to consider deep penetration beyond the Meuse bridgehead. General Ernst Busch did not even think that Guderian would manage to cross the Meuse at all while General von Bock, commander of Army Group B, assigned the attack in the Lowlands, told Halder:

"You will be creeping along, ten miles from the Maginot line flank on your breakthrough and hoping that the French will watch inertly. You are cramming the mass of tanks together into the narrow roads of the Ardennes as if there were no such thing as air power. And you then hope to lead an operation as far as the coast with an open southern flank, 200 miles long, where stands the mass of the French Army."[2]

Under this veil of skepticism the war games were held. Guderian and Wietersham, commanding the XIV Motorized Corps, stood firm in their insistence that the Panzer Divisions not be split.

The subsequent exercise demonstrated beyond doubt the feasibility of Guderian's proposal and proved the icing on the cake of the Manstein plan. Albeit reluctantly, Halder was now compelled to offer his blessing.

Therefore, the now approved Manstein plan called for Army Group B under von Bock, with 2 Armies and 3 Panzer Divisions, to advance into Belgium and Holland, thereby drawing the French and British forces forward to deal with the threat. Once accomplished, Army Group A, under von Rundstedt, would strike into the Allied rear via the Ardennes Forest of southern Belgium. The latter Army Group would consist of Fourth Army (General Gunther von Kluge), Sixteenth Army (General Ernst Busch), and Twelfth Army (General Sigmund List). The Panzers were divided into two corps under the overall command of General Ewald von Kleist and assigned to List's Twelfth Army.

Von Kleist was one of the old guard of the German Army officers and had virtually no previous experience in handling mobile formations. He was therefore an unusual choice for this role. Although his unfamiliarity with tank theories resulted in excessive caution during the battle for France, he later became (in Russia) one of Germany's most successful and brilliant armoured commanders.

Panzer Group Kleist was comprised of XLI Panzer Corps under General Hans Georg Reinhardt with the 6th and 8th Panzer Divisions and XIX Panzer Corps under Guderian with the 1st, 2nd and 10th Panzer Divisions. Also included in Kleist's command was the aforementioned XIV Motorized Corps whose role was to follow up Guderian's advance. XIX Panzer Corps would be the German's southernmost and as such, more likely to have its flank threatened.

With Hitler's acceptance of the plan, all that remained was its implementation. Its boldness appealed to Hitler and the promise of quick victory captivated his imagination. With the original plan having fallen into French hands, this more daring plan was ideally suited for Hitler's ambitions for European domination.

Now that the strategic concept was firmly agreed upon by all parties, Guderian feverishly set about readying his corps for the forthcoming battle. Arrangements were concluded with the Luftwaffe for their close cooperation and it was emphasized that close personal contact with the ground forces was imperative. The Luftwaffe command was briefed in deepest detail of the plans for crossing the Meuse and of their role in pinning down the French defenders at Sedan.

With the air support now assured, Guderian drew his corps into line abreast and, gathering his three divisional commanders (Kirchner, 1st Panzer, Veiel, 2nd Panzer, and Schaal, 10th Panzer), he attempted to instill his beliefs on them. He transmitted a feeling of absolute confidence, the sign of an outstanding leader. He told them that the commander must lead from the front and that the spearheads must be constantly kept moving.

Preparations were now complete and the green light to begin the offensive was awaited with eager anticipation. But one question continued to nag at the Germans. How would the French react? Hitler himself had experienced the French soldier during the First World War and found them to be hard, determined and vigorous fighters. However, that had been more than twenty years ago. What about 1940? Most books analyzing why France succumbed in six weeks catalogue the many signs of French weakness; poor leadership, outmoded defensive tactics, and ostrichlike defensive dispositions. Realizing that the French Army of 1940 was but a poor representation of the Army of 1914, let us examine the French dispositions immediately prior to the German attack.

General Maurice Gamelin, the French

Commander-in Chief, had drawn his armies up in line abreast facing Belgium with their left flank secured by the English Channel coast. Manning this flank was the French Seventh Army with the British Expeditionary Force on it's immediate right. These were followed in turn by the French First, Ninth, and Second Armies, the latter two facing the Ardennes Forest. The remaining French Armies facing the German frontier from their positions in the vaunted Maginot Line. These, upon commencement of the battle, would be tied down by a demonstration against their positions by the German Army Group "C" under General Ritter von Leeb.

It was highly unlikely that Guderian could have been aware that both the French Ninth and Second Armies, those directly in his path, were among the weakest in the entire French Army with the bulk of their formations consisting of newly formed divisional reserve units, overage veterans, and other troops of dubious quality at best.

On the fog shrouded morning of May 10, 1940, the German Blitzkrieg was unleashed. Guderian accompanied the 1st Panzer Division as it started into Luxembourg. By evening, the Belgian frontier had been crossed by the advance guard. That same evening Kleist, being more conservative, ordered 10th Panzer to assume a more southerly course in order to stave off a potential French threat from that sector. Guderian considered the order unwarrented and cancelled it immediately. To divert one-third of his corps for a hypothetical threat would too weaken his breakthrough and was considered absurd. Thus, he directed the commander of the 10th Panzer Division to continue westward. In any event, the threat never did materialize.

On the following day, XIX Corps cleared the Belgian border obstacles and were headed for the French frontier. As the advance continued unhindered, Sedan was rapidly approached. On May 12, 1st and 10th Panzer Divisions assaulted this ancient city and by evening the historic town was secured.

Meanwhile, Bock's attack in the Lowlands had produced precisely the desired effect. Anticipating a repeat of the World War I Schlieffen Plan, Gamelin's entire defensive strategy hinged on meeting this threat head on and was designated the "Dyle Plan". The movement forward into Belgium by the Allied Armies played right into German hands and left the rear ripe for a rapid advance westward. The French High Command expressed little concern for the eventuality of an attack through the Sedan area for it was concluded that any threat at this point could be easily dealt with by an attack from the North which would squeeze the enemy against the Maginot Line.

Kleist meanwhile issued orders for XIX Corps to launch their assault across the Meuse on the 13th. Guderian was a bit hesitant as 2nd Panzer had been delayed and had yet to arrive on the scene. Furthermore, Guderian had just been involved in an unruffling experience when, on a

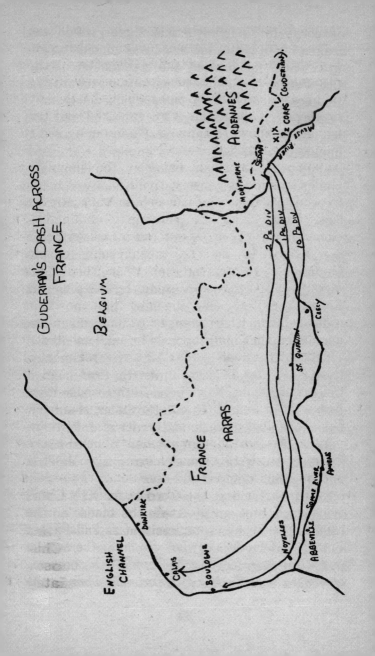

GUDERIAN'S DASH ACROSS FRANCE

ENGLISH CHANNEL

BELGIUM

FRANCE

ARRAS

Ardennes

Montherme

Sedan

XIX
Pz Corps (Guderian)

Meuse River

2 Pz Div

1 Pz Div

10 Pz Div

Cassy

St. Quentin

Dunkirk

Calais

Boulogne

Noyelles

Abbeville

Somme River

Amiens

return flight from a meeting with Kleist, his pilot lost direction and nearly came down in the French lines. It was only Guderian's quick recognition of their actual location which saved them. How would the subsequent battle have proceeded if Guderian were captured? History will never know. Despite all, Guderian agreed to launch the attack.

Inevitably a clash between the impulsive Guderian and the conservative Kleist was bound to occur. At this point it was over Luftwaffe tactics. Kleist and the Luftwaffe commander, General Hugo Sperrle, ordered a massed bombing attack to precede the crossing despite Guderian's recommendation that the planes merely support the crossing by keeping the French artillery and machine gun positions pinned down. Kleist refused to back down and demanded that his proposals be implemented.

On the afternoon of May 13, a rifle regiment of the 1st Panzer Division under the command of Colonel Hermann Balck crossed the Meuse River just west of Sedan. Thanks to the excellent rapport established with the Luftwaffe units involved, the local air commander, General Bruno Loerzer, stuck to Guderian's original directive and used his fighters and dive bombers to great effect in attacking the French defensive positions each time an attempt was made to man them. The result completely demoralized the French defenders who found themselves powerless to affect the outcome of the crossing and were soon fleeing in panic. Ironically, tank terror which had undermined German morale in 1917–18, was now turned upon its originators. French infantrymen fled from key, and in many cases, unthreatened positions at the mere hint of a tanks engine, though at times some of the engine's they heard were from their own units.

Throughout the night, Balck continued to apply pressure and by morning of the 14th, advance elements of his units were ten miles beyond the Meuse.

Meanwhile, French General George's Northwest Command which encompassed all the armies of Northern France, had perceived the attack at Sedan and issued orders for three French armoured divisions to counterattack the German spearheads. On the 14th, the 3rd French Armoured Division which was the closest, was thrown into the attack piecemeal and were chewed up in detail by the 1st and 10th Panzer Divisions resulting in heavy French losses. The attack did however cause Guderian to be concerned with the exposure of his southern flank.

In the wake of Balck's spectacular coup, Guderian ordered pontoon bridges constructed over the Meuse and, adhering to his doctrine of leading from the front, rushed the 1st and 2nd Panzer Divisions over the river in the face of British and French air attacks. Guderian fearlessly accompanied the leading elements of the advance.

"I went over in the first assault boat. On the far bank I found the efficient and brave commander of the 1st Rifle Regiment, Lt. Colonel Balck, together with his staff. He greeted me cheerfully with the cry: Joy riding in canoes on the Meuse is forbidden! I had in fact used those words myself in one of the exercises that we had in preparation for the operation, since the attitude of some of the younger officers had struck me as rather too light-hearted. I now realized that they had judged the situation correctly."[3]

Meanwhile, off to the North, the Corps commanded by Reinhardt and another under General Hermann Hoth had caved in the front of French General Corap's Ninth Army at Dinant. Both corps continued their advance westward in the face of a confused and panic stricken enemy. The rout of Corap's command effectively wrote the end of any thought of the possibility of a French attack into the Sedan bridgehead from the North.

By evening of the 14th, the German bridgehead was fifteen miles deep and thirty miles wide. The left wing of the French Second Army was completely destroyed and the depressed French General Georges issued orders for the formations remaining at Sedan to withdraw. These forces by this point had been thoroughly routed, so that Georges had little choice.

During the planning stages for the attack, the question arose concerning Guderian's intentions once the bridgehead was secure and the breakout from Sedan realized. The Panzer Leader stated that he would not stop, but rather would continue the advance towards Amiens and upon reaching that objective his forces could be turned southwards towards Paris or continue on to the channel coast.

On the 15th, the push westward resumed. Guderian was still concerned about his southern flank (the northern flank was protected by Reinhardt's advance) so he turned the 10th Panzer Division over to Wietersham's command in order to assist the latter in guarding the bridgehead until it could be properly secured.

On this same day, French President Paul Reynaud phoned his counterpart in England, Prime Minister Winston Churchill, and flatly stated, "We have been defeated, we are beaten and have lost the battle." Guderian's master stroke had completely sown the seeds of defeat.

On the evening of the 15th, just as XIX Corps was preparing to expand the bridgehead, von Kleist ordered Guderian to suspend any further westward advance until the bridgehead was secured.

After a heated exchange during which Guderian said in disgust, "I neither would nor could agree to these orders, which involved the sacrifice of the element of surprise we had gained."[4] Kleist reluctantly granted permission to continue the advance for another twenty-four hours.

On the morning of the 16th, 1st and 2nd Panzer Divisions once again set out westward.

The former ran into heavy opposition near Bouvellemont but Balck's regiment managed to overcome the French defences in some of the heaviest fighting to date. With Guderian urging them on from his command vehicle, both divisions penetrated past Montcourt where they linked up with the 6th Panzer Division of Reinhardt's Corps. By nightfall, the spearheads of XIX Corps were fifty miles beyond Sedan. Wietersham, confident of his ability to defend the southern flank now that the opposition was flattened, returned 10th Panzer Division to Guderian's operational control.

Once again the boom was lowered on Guderian. Before operations could resume on the 17th, Kleist once more ordered a complete halt and directed Guderian to report to Panzergruppe Headquarters. It seemed that the German High Command was unable to comprehend how swiftly their dreams of rapid conquest were becoming a reality. General Halder noted that even the Feuhrer appeared frightened by his own success and was worried about the southern flank. Thus, he would not allow any further westward movement. It seemed that everything that Guderian had so long tried to hammer home, that once a panzer thrust got going, it must above all keep moving so that the enemy would be continuously subjected to constant attack and rendered unable to organize a counterattack, had fallen on deaf ears.

Guderian, of course, was furious. Upon his arrival at Panzergruppe Headquarters, Kleist berated the former for disobeying orders by advancing beyond the parameters previously outlined. Guderian, never known for his diplomacy, lost his temper and offered his resignation on the spot. Kleist readily accepted and ordered the command turned over to the senior divisional commander, Veiel of 2nd Panzer Division.

Von Rundstedt however, would have none of it and dispatched List, commander of Twelfth Army to smooth things over. This List accomplished and with tongue in cheek, authorized Guderian to conduct a "reconnaissance in force." It was expressly stipulated however that Guderian was to remain at his headquarters and was not to accompany the forward troops on their mad dash to the coast. "This was at least something",[5] as he agreed. However, he then proceeded to simply lay a telephone wire from his rear area headquarters to wherever he happened to be at the time. In this way, he was able to maintain contact with his own headquarters without having to resort to radio communications whose transmissions were subject to interception by his superiors.

Meanwhile, that evening, 1st Panzer Division reached the banks of the Oise near St. Quentin and crossed the river that night, establishing a bridgehead.

Halder, in a complete about face, abandoned his scepticism over the threat to Guderian's southern flank, a feeling which was not shared by Hitler and von Rundstedt. The Chief of the

General Staff however, was considering an attack south towards Paris and the rear of the Maginot Line; this he felt would end any threat from that point.

During the 18th, 1st and 2nd Panzer Divisions enlarged the bridgehead over the Oise and managed to advance to within fifty miles of the channel near Abbeville. While the advance was proceeding in earnest, the Commander-in-Chief of the Army, General von Brauchitsch, overturned the reconnaissance in force directive and gave the panzers license to proceed at will.

Early the next morning, Guderian's troops forced a bridgehead over the Somme at Peronne. With that, he then ordered 1st Panzer to Amiens while directing 2nd Panzer to Abbeville.

Needless to say, the French command was in a state of utter panic. They sacked General Gamelin and replaced him with General Maxime Weygand, a man of more forceful personality.

The appointment of Weygand as Gamelin's successor was an action long overdue, but was an act of a drowning man grasping for straws. The aging general's arrival did breathe new life into the French High Command and restore a level of confidence and enthusiasm but by this point, France was beyond saving.

Meanwhile, General Bilotte, one of France's more capable commanders, was ordered to assemble the remnants of the shattered French armies fighting in southern Belgium. His mission called for an attack southward to sever the head of the German attack. Returning to his headquarters, Bilotte's staff car was involved in a collision that cost the general his life and destroyed any remaining hope. Weygand opted for going over to the offensive. Though conceived in desperation, it is doubtful that his plan could have succeeded for, by this time, List's Twelfth Army and Kluge's Fourth Army had moved forward to plug the void created by the rapid advance of the panzers. The planned attack southward would almost certainly have been shattered against the wall of defence thrown up by the two German armies.

While all this was transpiring, the Panzer Divisions of Guderian's, Hoth's and Reinhardt's were drawn into line abreast forming a seven division wide spearhead that pushed forward, brushing aside all in its path. Guderian was in his element. His propaganda officer, Paul Diericks had this to say about Guderian.

"He radiates a sensation of positive and personal calmness. He is never ruffled. But that does not mean that Guderian cannot astonish his officers. For instance, when he arrives at a command post of a subordinate unit and states it's next task, many a person might think it a joke that the goal would be placed so far ahead. But in short, clear terms, the general explains the feasibility of the operation. At such moments he speaks in a fascinating way to put over his intense desire to advance."[6]

This was his element, to boldly advance, to mow down all in his path.

Amiens fell to Kirchner on the 20th while Veiel, after capturing Albert, pushed his forward elements into and beyond Abbeville that same evening. By nightfall, the exhausted troopers of the 2nd Panzer Division found themselves staring out over the English Channel. The race to the coast had been won. Abbeville was secured during the night of May 20-21, and now XIX Corps settled down, regrouping itself and waiting further orders from higher command.

Late in the day of the 21st, orders were received to advance on the channel ports. Guderian, however, was fuming because of the procrastination exhibited by higher command. One whole day of campaigning was wasted while General Headquarters decided which approach to take. Finally, upon receipt of the orders, Guderian directed 10 Panzer to Dunkirk, 1st Panzer to Calais and 2nd Panzer to Bolougne.

Kleist again proved to be a thorn in Guderian's side. Though later one of Hitler's more successful commanders, during the dash to the coast he appeared to lack the knowledge regarding the role of armoured formations and lacked the confidence and enthusiasm for the operation which was more than compensated for by Guderian's diametric approach. Because of this, Kleist contributed to a series of delays that were detrimental to the objectives of the panzers and merely served to give the French breathing space. His distaste for Guderian also contributed

Luftwaffe their moment in the sun. After all, the Luftwaffe was more steeped in National Socialist tradition and ideology than the army. Still another theory claims that Hitler wished the British Expeditionary Force to escape so that the British would be more amenable to peace offers.

Whatever the theory or combination of same are correct is beside the point for there still remains the irrefutable fact, the might of the German Army, just as it was ready to attack Dunkirk and seal off any Allied means of escape, was held back at the crucial moment. Guderian's reaction to the order was curt; We were utterly speechless, but since we were not informed of the reason for this order, it was difficult to argue against it."[8]

Hitler, after a meeting with his chief advisors on the 25th, indicated that from now on, all further decisions were to be left to von Rundstedt. The latter ordered the infantry to close up behind the panzers, for he wanted the armoured formations to rest for the ordeal ahead. However, on the 26th, under heavy pressure, von Rundstedt lifted the stop order and informed all units to resume the attack. The Allies, having been granted a breathing spell from the armoured onslaught, used their time wisely by forming a strong defensive perimeter around Dunkirk into which poured the battered French and British units.

With the panzers once more on the move; they found the flooded countryside around Gravelines very troublesome, for the terrain was extremely difficult to traverse. Meeting such stiff resistance, the panzer generals lost their enthusiasm for continuing the attack.

On May 28, after making little headway, Guderian's corps was pulled out of line and ordered to stand down. The Corps of Hoth and Reinhardt followed suit the next day. The three corps were given orders to regroup on the Somme in anticipation of the final assault against the remaining French forces in metropolitan France.

Before abandoning the lines for his next assignment, Guderian found time to express his gratitude to the forces under his command. This took the form of the following Corps order.

"Soldiers of the XIX Army Corps. For seventeen days we have been fighting in Belgium and France. We have covered a good 400 miles since crossing the German border: we have reached the channel coast and the Atlantic Ocean. On the way here you have thrust through the Belgium fortifications, forced a passage of the Meuse, broken the Maginot Line extension in the memorable Battle of Sedan, captured the important heights of Stonne and then, without halt, fought your way through St. Quentin and Peronne to the lower Somme at Amiens and Abbeville. You have set the crown on your achievements by the capture of the channel coast and the sea fortresses of Bolougne and Calais. I asked you to go without sleep for 48 hours. You have gone for 17 days. I compelled you to accept risks to your flanks and rear. You never faltered. With masterly self-confidence and believing in the fulfillment of your mission, you carried out every order with devotion.

"Germany is proud of her Panzer Divisions, and I am happy to be your commander.

"We remember our fallen comrades with honor and respect, sure in the knowledge that their sacrifice was not in vain.

"Now we shall arm ourselves for new needs. For Germany and for our leader, Adolf Hitler.

Signed, Guderian"[9]

It had been a truly remarkable feat of arms which the Germans had accomplished. In less than two weeks, the reputedly most powerful army in Europe, the French, had been shattered and cast aside by a handful of divisions, brilliantly led, superbly trained, and highly dedicated.

Guderian's role cannot be minimized. His drive, boundless energy, brilliant tactics and confidence in his units had been the most significant part of this astonishing victory. Without a Guderian to argue with Kleist, to object violently to stop orders, to harass the divisions commanders into advancing at all cost, the results may have been decidedly different. He had forged the Panzer Divisions in the face of conservative opposition that thought him an impulsive madman. Then he led his creation in a remarkable victory, a type of victory that the Germans had relished for centuries. It is perhaps excusable that men such as Kleist, von Rundstedt, and Hitler were hesitant, for the swift victory handed to them by Guderian was beyond the realm of their wildest dreams.

The final battle for France was relatively anticlimactic. Guderian, rewarded with command of his own Panzergruppe, pushed his units down the Rhone valley before spreading out and compressing the defenders against the Maginot Line and the Swiss border with the units of Kleist on his right.

The collapse of France was complete. Guderian's Panzergruppe alone had taken approximately 250,000 prisoners plus an incalculable quantity of equipment of all sorts. Finally, on the 22 of June, the French Government, under the aged Marshal Petain, agreed to an armistice.

The conclusion of hostilities afforded the Wermacht time to refit and reorganize their command structure while affording them the time to learn the lessons of armoured tactics so recently demonstrated.

The soldiers fight, but the politicians make war. So Hitler continued to lead his country down this path. On June 22, 1941, Hitler unleashed his panzers again. But this time the opposition was supplied by the hated Bolsheviks. The Wermacht now boasted no less than four Panzergruppes.

The attack on the Soviet Union was conducted with three massive assault groups, Army Groups North, Center, and South respectively. Kleist's Panzergruppe was assigned to Army Group South, General Hoeppner's Panzergruppe was attached to Army Group North, while the 4th and 2nd Panzergruppes commanded by Hoth and Guderian respectively, spearheaded the drive of von Bock's Army Group Center on Moscow.

Cutting through like a hot knife through butter, Hoth and Guderian sliced into the Soviets, dismembering huge chunks of Russian territory. Dashing forward miles apart before converging on each other, the two Panzergruppes encircled 600,000 Russian troops when they met at Minsk. Another 300,000 went into the bag after Hoth and Guderian joined forces again at Smolensk. The speed of the advance had been breathtaking with some units of Panzergruppe 2 advancing as much as seventy miles in one day.

Many books have been written on what was now to take place. Only the thin threads of the story as they relate to Guderian can be unturned at this time. In late August, Hitler changed his strategy and decided that the advance of Army Group South under von Rundstedt which was pointed at the Ukraine, must take priority. Against Guderian's better judgement, he was ordered south to assist von Rundstedt. On September 15th, Guderian's advance units met Kleist's who were striking northward at Lokhvistsa, sealing off 500,000 hapless Soviet soldiers in the Kiev pocket.

With von Rundstedt's attack exceeding expectations, Guderian was once more ordered to drive on Moscow. Unfortunately for the Germans, after the long months of continuous campaigning, the panzers were worn out and in need of refit and repair. It was therefore impossible to resume the advance immediately, resulting in an even further postponement of a major attack towards Moscow.

Among other difficulties confronting Guderian was the attitude of von Kluge, commander of the Fourth Army, to whom Guderian's forces were nominally subordinate. Kluge, jealous of Guderian's success and still unable to grasp the lessons of France, was reluctant to allow Guderian freedom of movement and sufficient latitude for independent decisions. These inexcusable restrictions dictated by von Kluge resulted in severe friction between the two and led to an abrasive working relationship at best.

In addition, Russian opposition was displaying signs of stiffening. Although Guderian managed to penetrate beyond Moscow to the South, the onset of the severe Russian winter thwarted all German attempts at capturing the Soviet capital. While Hitler's soldiers were freezing on the steps of Russia, his generals were in violent disagreement over the Fuhrer's order to stand fast rather than withdrawing to prepared winter positions.

Though Guderian felt that Moscow should be taken for many reasons, such as its key position as an industrial complex and center of road and rail systems and the psychological effect it would have on both Russia and Germany, he realistically saw that the city could not be taken in 1941 and he relayed this opinion to Hitler. Those bold enough to propose a retreat and then order a withdrawal despite orders to the contrary received a suitable reward from Hitler; loss of command. Foremost among those who sacrificed their commands were von Rundstedt, von Bock and Guderian. On December 26, 1941, Guderian, the architect of so many spectacular German victories, was assigned to the reserve officers pool; literally an unemployed officer.

It is not the intent of this chapter to review Guderian's career in its entirety. Suffice it to recall that upon the reversal of German fortunes, Hitler decided that he could no longer do without the services of his finest armoured tactician. So, in 1943, Guderian was recalled and appointed Inspector General of Panzer Troops, making him responsible for the development, organization, and training of all armoured units.

Guderian opposed the German offensive at Kursk and shortly after that hapless battle, retired to his sick bed with a severe cardiac problem. Later in the year, he attempted to persuade General Alfred Jodl to reorganize the supreme command so that a new Commander-in-Chief of the Army would lessen Hitler's direct influence on the actual conduct of operations. It was to little avail. Jodl's retort was: "Do you know of a better commander than Adolf Hitler?"[10]

With the failure of the assassination attempt

against Hitler on July 20, 1944, Guderian replaced General Kurt Zeitzler as Chief of the General Staff. In this role, Guderian, impulsive and headstrong as ever, refused to allow Hitler to intimidate him and argued his cause with the latter whenever necessary.

The only blemish on Guderian's illustrious career was his chairmanship of the Army Tribunal which dismissed from the service those military members who were actively involved in the conspiracy against Hitler. This action allowed those officers to be tried by a civilian court. It was not however, an assignment that Guderian relished or desired but one demanded of him by virtue of his position as Chief of the General Staff.

Finally, in March of 1945, after a particularly violent disagreement, Hitler sent Guderian on sick leave, using the latter's heart condition as an excuse. He did however, make Guderian promise to remain available for future employment at short notice. Before he could actually be recalled, the war was over.

With the end of the war, Guderian was detained by the Allies as a war criminal but in June of 1947, he was informed that all charges were dropped and he was allowed to retire to his home where he died peacefully in 1951.

Would France have fallen so swiftly had someone other than Guderian been in command? It seems highly unlikely. As evidenced by the attitudes of Kleist and von Rundstedt and even the Fuhrer, only Guderian truly comprehended the ability of tanks to move with such speed and destruction. His tactic of leading from the front and prodding the tottering and lethargic commanders, inspired these commanders to continue to advance despite their traditional fear of threat to their flanks and rear. Guderian was a necessary factor.

Later Hoth, Hoeppner, Rommel, Reinhardt and yes, even Kleist, were to bring Guderian's tactics to a high level of proficiency.

Did other countries produce leaders as audacious as Guderian? America's Patton probably most effectively imitated the aggressiveness of Guderian. He definitely made use of the tactics devised and practiced by Guderian. Many of the American armoured commanders right down to divisional level made excellent use of his teachings.

Of the British, it appears that only General O'Connor was audacious enough to adopt Guderian's tactics.

France was most certainly Guderian's masterpiece. Without the victory created by the dash of the panzers from Sedan, the war may have dragged on for months with consequences that may have been devastating to the Germans.

Was he Germany's best General? Perhaps. Liddell-Hart has commented that he possessed all the qualities that distinguish great captains of history. "He combined acute observation with sure intuition, had an ability to create surprise and throw an opponent off balance, speed of thought and action, and a combination of strategic and tactical sense coupled with a power to capture the devotion of his troops."[11]

However, we must remember Guderian was a specialist and as such, had a tendency to look with scepticism on other branches of the service. The jury in this case must remain forever out, for Guderian, bold and daring as he was, never commanded in the field forces other than Panzers. Perhaps if he were required to command infantry and artillery along with tanks, his tactics would have required modification. His concerns would then, by necessity, have had to broaden. Thus history will be left to draw her own conclusions.

Field Marshal Karl Rudolf Gerd von Rundstedt, next to Erwin Rommel and Heinz
Guderian, was one of the most notarized and
respected German Generals of World War II.
Yet, he did not create any new military theory,
strategy, or tactic. We can all recall the name of
von Schlieffen of pre-World War I fame with his
master plan for defeating France, or von Manstein for the plan which did defeat France during
six short weeks in 1940. But von Rundstedt did
not create any master plan or doctrine of war.
Yet, three months prior to the beginning of
Hitler's historic and fateful attack on Poland,
von Rundstedt, who had retired seven months
previously at the age of sixty-three and at the
height of his career, was recalled to active duty
by Hitler. Why did the latter feel the need to
recall this aged warrior?

The choice of von Rundstedt was made by
Hitler personally. What attracted the General to
the man who held the German Generals in such
contempt and was critical of them? Though a
loyal German, he was not a party member and
certainly no toady. In fact, he typified the classic
Prussian aristocrat who looked down his nose

upon the common background of Hitler and the vulgarity of the Nazi Party.

Nor did von Rundstedt create any new Panzer doctrine. On the contrary, being a veteran member of the Great German General Staff, he had a tendency to lean more to the tenants of orthodoxy:

What made the difference was experience, and in this Hitler was not to be disappointed by his choice. In the short span of two years, von Rundstedt would lead German armies to great victories in Poland, France, and Russia until the onset of the Soviet winter created new problems for the great old man. By examining these three campaigns and the later defense of Europe, the authors would like to portray von Rundstedt's commanding ability.

For many commanders under the conditions of Hitler's Reich, independent leadership was most difficult and in many instances, virtually impossible. During the Polish and French campaigns and for part of the 1941 Russian campaign, he was able to make major decisions of his own within the broad framework of the directives from Army High Command and so was able to lay the foundation of his reputation. In time, however, initiative and independence were wrest from his hand as more and more Hitler began to personally direct the war.

Gerv von Rundstedt was descended from a very long line of Prussian soldiers stretching back to the twelfth century. He inherited all the dignity and pride due his aristocratic type. A portrait of von Rundstedt's parents in 1874 portray the dignity of their station. His father is dressed in the uniform of a lieutenant in a Prussian Hussar Regiment and his mother's dignified face characterizes a woman of high-born background. Into this heritage young Gerd was born on December 12, 1875.

At age twelve, he became a cadet at Oranienstein, a military boarding school where his instructors noted quite early his intelligence and his ability with languages. At sixteen, he graduated to the Central Prussian Cadet College at Gross Lichterfelde near Berlin. In 1892, after passing qualifying exams, he was accepted into the German Army with the rank of ensign. Next followed the process of choosing a regiment which in reality turned out to be which regiment would accept his application. Although hoping to be accepted into the cavalry, he settled for the infantry when he found his application accepted by the 83rd Infantry Regiment von Wittlich.

His first service was at Kassel where he served six months in officer training. Upon completion of this course and the successful passage of the necessary exams, he was commissioned a second-lieutenant in June of 1893.

The young lieutenant then found himself assigned to the headquarters of the 83rd at Kassel. In 1896 he was posted to Arolesen and in 1900 found himself again at Kassel where two years later he married Louise von Gotz, daughter of a retired officer. During his courtship, he found time to take the qualifying examinations for admission to the Staff College. Acceptance at the Staff College was vital for any young officer desiring promotion, particularly if he were seeking a future appointment to the Great General Staff. Von Rundstedt of course desired both promotion and an appointment to the General Staff.

At the Staff College, von Rundstedt excelled in tactics. His ability virtually assured him a General Staff appointment and so, in 1906, he was rewarded with appointment as a probationer of the Great German General Staff. With the passage of a rigorous exam, in March, 1909, he became a captain of the General Staff.

His initial staff appointment was at the head-quarters of the XI Corps. There was wide-spread acceptance of the theory that staff officers would better carry out their duties if they served with a regiment and learned first hand the problems of the various units. In this way, they would not lose touch with the fighting soldier. Thus it was common practice to rotate staff officers, giving them regimental duties followed by other staff appointments. As a result, in September, 1912, von Rundstedt became a company commander in the 171st regiment.

August 1914 brought war to Europe and a staff appointment for von Rundstedt. His title was 1A, Chief operations officer of the 22nd Reserve Division and was the most prestigious staff appointment to which a mere captain could be assigned. Not until November would he be promoted to the rank of major.

Von Rundstedt's primary command responsibility was to bring this reserve division up to the level of a war footing. First, he was required to have the division concentrated at Dusseldorf which was accomplished on August 10. It was then moved by road to Aachen and shortly into combat in Belgium. The first serious action came during the Battle of the Marne during which the divisional commander was seriously wounded leaving command to the young captain. Eye witnesses reported that he portrayed calm, deliberate leadership under fire.

After the war stagnated to trench warfare, von Rundstedt left the 22nd to take up a staff position with the German Military Goverment of Belgium. Though it was German practice to rotate staff officers from regimental to staff duties, during time of war this practice was for all intent and purpose abandoned and staff officers were theoretically required to serve only at headquarters. To sacrifice a well trained staff officer in combat was believed to be a waste of strategical talent. Thus, for the rest of the war, von Rundstedt found himself involved in staff work, first on the Military Governor of Belgium's staff, then with the Military Government in Warsaw, a Corps in the Carpathians, another Corps on the Baltic coast and finally, near war's end, as Chief of Staff of the XV Corps on the Western Front.

On November 11, 1918, the day of shame for the German Army, von Rundstedt was faced with an uncertain future. With the ratification of the punitive Treaty of Versailles, the German Army was reduced to a mere 100,000 men. The Reichswehr, as the new Army was called, was organized by General Hans von Seeckt, a man of exceptional ability. He had clear ideas who should become a part of this army. Who to select for appointment to this army was a most difficult decision for the German Army was staffed by many exceptional soldiers. Von Seeckt wished to attract a large proportion of aristocratic officers with his chief concern being to retain as many General Staff officers as possible. As Seeckt himself had said:

"We must look first of all to experienced General Staff Officers."[1]

Von Rundstedt ideally fit the type of officer for this new Reichswehr. He was a nobleman of the old Prussian lineage who could trace his ancestry back centuries. Members of his family had fought for William of Orange against the Spaniards and with Charles I in Scotland. Not only that, his father was a former Prussian officer and von Rundstedt himself was a member of the General Staff. In October, 1920, as part of the 100,000 man army, he was promoted to Lt. Colonel and appointed Chief of Staff to the 3rd Cavalry Division.

Von Seekct set as an important policy for the German Army, its status above party and state. It was to be immune from political involvement and would back any government which preserved the unity of the German people and provided provisions for the defense of the German frontier. He stated that the Army would not condone attempts by the soldiers to overthrow the government by force. This attitude was adopted wholeheartedly by von Rundstedt.

In 1923, he was promoted full Colonel and by the end of the year was transferred from the 3rd Cavalry Division to Headquarters of Wehrkreis II as its Chief of Staff. Two years later, he became commander of the 18th Infantry Regiment. In 1926 he again returned to staff duty as Chief of Staff of Obergruppenkommando II at Kassel. He was then promoted major-general and posted as divisional commander of the 2nd Cavalry Division. In 1929, he was promoted Lt. General and in January, 1932, was made General Officer Commanding Wehrkreis III in Berlin. By October of the same year, he had been promoted to full General and was named the commander of Obergruppenkommando I in Berlin, the highest post outside of the War Ministry to which an officer could aspire.

It was in this position that von Rundstedt found himself in 1933 when the course of German history was radically altered. Adolf Hitler and his band of street brawling Nazi Party thugs had, since the onset of the world depression, gradually become the dominant political party in Germany. Though the army was sworn to remain aloof from political involvement, many young soldiers had, since the 1920's, leaned towards the Nazi party, finding its appeal infectious, particularly the message of German greatness.

On January 30, 1933, Adolf Hitler was chosen by the aged Reich President, Field Marshal von Hindenburg, as chancellor of Germany. As Chancellor, Hitler was resolved that no one would control him and within a short time was able to gain full dictatorial control of the country. He realized, however, that this could not be accomplished without the full support of the Army and by mid-February, 1933, a mere two weeks after becoming Chancellor, he was able to obtain the Army's support for elections to be held by promising the Generals that their tradition of non-political involvement was safe in his hands. Soon after, the Reichstag was burned and an Enabling Act was passed giving Hitler dictatorial power to deal with the suspected Communist revolution. Now, all power was usurped by Hitler and his party. The only institution in the German State which Hitler did not yet dominate was the Army.

Though unable to wield control over the Reichswehr, Hitler found ways to curb its effectiveness and influence in the state. He professed to the generals his desire for a bigger army, the prospect of which appealed to the military men. One major obstacle preventing the Army from throwing its full support behind Hitler was the existance of the Sturmabterlungen, the S.A. This latter represented to the German Army a dire threat to its autonomy. The General worried that Hitler would order the S.A. and the Reichswehr to be merged into one Army under

Nazi leadership. If the army Hitler advocated was to be made up of the non aristocratic, boorish, street-fighting brownshirted S.A., then the Generals would have little choice but to resist tooth and nail.

Little action was taken for a year but in 1934, with von Hindenburg nearing death at the ripe old age of eighty-five, Hitler was forced to make some very important decisions. He desired to make himself President upon the old man's death but to do this he required the open support of the German Army since the presidency carried with it the honorary title of Chief of the Armed Forces. If it meant dismemberment, surely the Army would oppose him.

Hitler was thus forced to choose between purging the S.A. and opposing some of his old cronies or defying the Army and taking his chances. He chose the path which held the greatest prospect for success. On June 30, 1934, the 'Night of the Long Knives,' Hitler disciplined the S.A, had Ernst Rohm, its head, killed and reduced the whole status of the S.A. thus indicating to the Army that it was they who were the sole Armed Forces of the German State. In August, 1934, Hindenburg died and Hitler became President of Germany and Chief of the Armed Forces.

During these early days of Hitler's rule, von Rundstedt found himself stationed in Berlin. The Commander-in-Chief of the Army at this time was General Werner von Fritsch with General Ludwig Beck as Chief of the General Staff. Both of these officers were not in Hitler's favor and although their opposition to his policies were well known, they lived relative reclusive lives. Von Rundstedt, who was next in line senioritywise behind these two officers was thus given the responsibility for social leadership. His house became the center for much entertainment of foreign diplomats and military guests that the Army was required to provide.

1935 saw many changes in the German Army. Its name was officially changed from Reichswehr to Wermacht and all its members were now required to swear their allegiance not to the German state, but to the German Fuhrer. In the same year, it began to grow in size as Hitler threw out the punitive clauses of the Treaty of Versailles which had limited the German Army to no more than 100,000 men.

Gradually, the Army found itself coming more and more under the influence of Hitler. His bravado in the Rhineland had filled the Army with pride even though not all the military leaders were overly enthused with his leadership. Always seeking methods of bringing the Army more under his control, in 1938 Hitler made his move upon receipt of damaging and distasteful information against his two Army leaders, War Minister Werner von Blomberg and General von Fritsch. The former had reportedly embarassed the Army and compromised its reputation by marrying a woman of ill repute with Hitler and Goering as his witnesses. Commander-in-Chief Fritsch was falsely accused of being a homosexual. Blomberg resigned his position immediately and the unfortunate von Fritsch was sacked after a brief but unsuccessful effort to save his reputation. Ever the loyal Hitlerite, von Blomberg suggested to Hitler that he assume the post of War Minister himself rather than waste time in an effort to find someone compatable. Thus Hitler reorganized the High Command with all ministerial functions passing into his hands but managed by General (later Field Marshal) Wilhelm Keitel. Fritsch's post was handed to General Walther von Brauchitsch. Both Beck and von Runstedt protested this situation vehemently, particularly the shabby treatment of von Fritsch, but in vain.

The festering European situation boded ill for Beck who, along with other generals feared war as Hitler annexed Austria in March of 1938 and ranted and raged against Czechoslovakia. The British appeasement at Munich pulled the rug out from any nascent opposition within the Army ranks. The outcome of the Sudeten affair however, provided von Rundstedt with a convenient opportunity to take his retirement. In March 1938 he was promoted Colonel General and found himself the most senior officer in the Army. On November 1, 1938, at the age of sixty-three, he left the Army and retired with his wife to Kassel. His long and illustrious military career was, for all intents and purposes, over.

Retirement however, for von Rundstedt was to become illusive. On June 1, 1939, he was officially to the colors. Even before the official notification of recall was issued, a working staff called

"Working Staff von Rundstedt" had already prepared the groundwork for an operation on the Eastern frontier. One of the key officers on that staff was the brilliant General Erich von Manstein. Von Rundstedt, as superb military strategist, pushed himself wholeheartedly into the planning for 'Case White', as the proposed attack against the hated Polish was designated.

Von Rundstedt was assigned command of Army Group South with von Manstein as his Chief-of-Staff. This Army Group was comprised of the Eighth, Tenth, and Fourteenth Armies. Included in these armies were twelve corps, one of which was armoured. Eighth Army under General Johannes Blaskowitz contained X and XII Corps, Fourteenth Army commanded by General Sigmund List was made up of VIII, XVII, XXII, and XVIII Corps, while General Walther von Reichenau's Tenth Army contained XIV, XI, and XVI Armoured Corps, the latter under the command of General Erich Hoeppner.

With the plans for the invasion of Poland completed, the only determining factor remaining was the attitude of the British and French. Would they or would they not honor their commitment to Poland and fight if the German's precipitated war? If Germany were successful in isolating Poland from British and French aid, then Hitler could declare war and repossess the lands stolen from Germany at Versailles. Only Hitler's diplomatic skills could determine the course of the future and in August, 1939, he made his move. Sensing that Britain and France would be hard pressed to withdraw their guarantee to Poland, he wooed Russia over to the German side in hopes that the Western nations would see the futility of opposing German moves into Poland and allowing the Germans to fulfill their destiny.

Unbelievable as it may appear, France and Britain, by not responding to Soviet overtures for an alliance, pushed Russia firmly into an alliance with Germany culminating in the signing, on August 23, 1939, of a non-aggression pact. Though Communism and Nazism were politically opposed to each other, Stalin and Hitler both desired the security of the other's non-aggression. This security was thus made expedient for Soviet purposes. Isolation of Poland and the avoidance of a two front war made the pact expedient for Germany. At a conference with his generals on August 22, Hitler stated:

"The enemy had another hope that Russia would become our enemy. The enemy did not count on my power of resolution. Our enemies are little worms. I saw them at Munich. I have struck this weapon, the help of Russia, out of the hands of the western powers. The possibility now exists to strike at the heart of Poland. We need not fear a blockade. The east will supply us with grain, cattle, coal, lead and zinc . . . I am only afraid that, at the last moment some schweinhund will make a proposal for mediation . . . now that I have made the political preparations, the way is open for the soldier."[2]

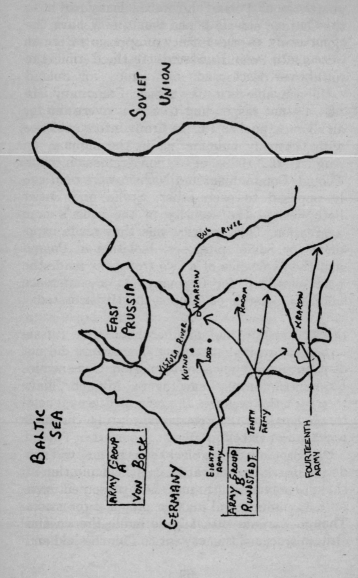

Von Rundstedt's reaction was that of a German nationalist who felt that Germany had been wronged at Versailles and would now have the opportunity to right the wrong done to it. At Nuremberg, von Rundstedt testified that the Nazi-Soviet Pact made him happy for Poland would not dare resist the might of Germany. He felt that another 'flower' war was in the offing, the same as in Austria, the Sudetenland, and the Rhineland.

On September 1, 1939, German forces crashed into Poland. The Luftwaffe was committed heavily, and by the second day, the Poles were driven from the skies. With the destruction of Polish air forces complete, the weight of the Luftwaffe was now diverted to support of the ground attack.

With the aid of Goering's pilots, the German Blitzkreig blasted its way through the meagre Polish defenses. Von Rundstedt's Army Group South found heavy opposition in upper Silesia and near the Polish city of Poznan and the industrial region encircling it. The determined Poles assembled their strongest forces and built their stoutest defenses in this region which cost the Germans heavy casualties during the first few days of fighting.

On September 3, the British and French declared war on Germany after the expiration of the ultimatum each country had presented upon official notification of Germany's aggression. Though war was officially declared, French and British troops were not sent to Poland's aid and the latter, feeling the brunt of the German Blitzkrieg, were forced to gradually fall back, first to Warsaw, then across the Vistula River.

Near Poznan, the German Eighth Army ran into such stiff Polish opposition that von Rundstedt had to personally intervene. General Blaskowitz, the Army commander, had seriously miscalculated the Polish Army's move. Thinking that the enemy was in headlong retreat, he moved his army eastward in order to cut it off. But the Poznan Army delayed its withdrawal leaving the Eighth Army's left flank dangerously exposed. Recognizing the plight of the Germans, the Polish commander capitalized on the situation and initiated a series of counterblows across the Bzura River. This potentially nasty situation was one that should never have occurred and was definitely not in the plan of the German High Command.

Von Rundstedt, accompanied by von Manstein, quickly flew to Lodz where he was able to assess Blaskowitz's plight and issue orders to rectify the sticky situation. He immediately ordered the transfer of 2nd Infantry Division from Tenth Army to Eighth Army sector and directed it to fill the gap between the latter's left and the border forces. Thus a crisis was averted. No sooner had his quick action cleared and untangled that mess when another emergency arose on his central sector.

According to OKH appreciation, the Polish Lodz and Pomeranian Armies were in headlong retreat to the Vistula River. Von Rundstedt, however, took exception to the view of OKH. Relying on information gathered by his reconnaissance units, he determined that the Poles were still present in great strength around Lodz and Radom and decided that swift action on his part would allow his forces to encircle the enemy west of Warsaw, forcing the destruction of a large number of Polish forces. Both General Brauchitsch, Commander-in-Chief of the Army and General Halder, Chief of Staff, after lengthy debate, agreed with von Rundstedt's appreciation and allowed Eighth Army and the bulk of Tenth Army to wheel northwards and abandon their northeasterly and easterly drive. To these armies fell the task of cutting off the Polish armies west of the Bug and Vistula Rivers and attacking the Polish forts blocking the Vistula which would then allow the river crossings to come under fire. This action launched a major battle to accomplish dual tasks. First the capture of Warsaw itself followed by the destruction and capitulation of the Polish central armies.

The ensuing battle, known as the battle of the Kutno pocket, began on September 11. Like a giant pincer, Eighth Army and Third Army from General Fedor von Bock's Army Group North, converged on Modlin and Warsaw. The desperate battle raged until September 27, during which time the beleagured Poles made several futile efforts to break the encirclement. One feeble attempt to break out did experience some initial success but the wretched Poles were then brought to battle by German supporting formations outside the pocket and destroyed. Finally, on September 27, 140,000 Poles, recognizing the hopelessness of their plight, threw down their arms and marched off into captivity.

While the battle of Kutno pocket raged, von Rundstedt did not stand idle. Tenth Army completed the destruction of the Polish forces south of Warsaw and in the section around Radom, while Fourteenth Army further south, smashed the enemy Carpathian Army.

By the conclusion of the Polish campaign, the battered Polish command found itself racked with confusion. On September 17, in keeping with the provisions of a secret protocol attached to the Nazi-Soviet pact, the Russian Army marched into Poland. Thus the Poles were caught in a vise between two giants as they sought in vain to establish a cohesive front. Unfortunately, one did not in fact exist. A few days later the situation stablized as the Soviet and German units fell back behind the previously designated demarcation lines, but by this time the Polish state was totally dissolved.

By mid-October, von Rundstedt had been relieved from command in the east and was reassigned to command Army Group A on the Western Front with his headquarters at Koblenz, on the Rhine River. He and his staff arrived and settled in on October 24.

For his intelligent conduct of the Polish campaign, Hitler rewarded von Rundstedt the Knight's Cross of the Iron Cross, the highest military award in Germany at the time. The recall of the 'old man' from retirement had paid handsome dividends for the Fuhrer. Experience did indeed pay off.

Von Rundstedt spent the winter of 1939-40 at Koblenz making preparations for Germany's next move. Two of his subordinates, Chief-of-Staff Manstein and Operations Officer General Gunther Blumentritt, had nothing but high praise for their military boss. Manstein commented that his chief had a distaste for matters of detail but:

"As an exponent of grand tactics, he was brilliant—a talented soldier who grasped the essentials of any problem in an instant."[3]

It was von Rundstedt's good fortune to be so ably served by such competent officers who concerned themselves with those matters not to von Rundstedt's liking.

That winter proved to be long and confusing. Although most history books refer to it as the period of the 'phoney war,' the Germans called the Sitzkreig. The big question was not whether the French and British would fight, but how and when would the Germans attack. Many plans were offered and discussed but none were implemented as the German High Command found ways of imposing postponement after postponement while the search for the best plan went on. It was even dared hope that Hitler could bring off another of his amazing political coups.

The original German plan for the defeat of France was a virtual carbon copy of the old Schlieffen Plan with Army Group B under von Bock effecting a swift drive from North German bases through the Netherlands and Belgium towards the coastal cities on the English Channel. Of the three German Army Groups, Army Group B was by far the strongest. Von Rundstedt's Army Group A meanwhile, being much weaker in strength, was ordered to support Bock's left flank. Though the plan was not popular with Hitler it was tentatively adopted. Many, however, felt the plan required drastic modification were it to succeed. This transformation originated in the headquarters of General von Rundstedt.

Along with OKH, von Rundstedt shared the conviction about the unsuitability of the plan and so stated in a letter to Brauchitsch on October 29, 1939, in which he stated:

"The success of the whole operation depends not on Bock's initial success in pushing back the Allied line in the north but on whether it will be possible completely to defeat and annihilate the enemy forces fighting there."[4]

In order to accomplish this, he went on to suggest that it would be necessary to move the center of effort (schwerpunkt) from Army Group B (Bock) to his own front. By doing so, he said, it would be possible for his forces to drive straight to the Channel coast at or below the line of the

Somme, thus cutting off the Allied forces which would be drawn northward by Bock's advance into Belgium. Both the danger and the chance of a great success would then lie in the hands of Army Group A. This plan was spawned in the mind of his brilliant Chief-of-Staff, von Manstein.

Von Rundstedt, however, was not totally committed to an offensive against the Western Allies. He feared that even if the British and French forces were defeated in Belgium, enough strength would still be available to resist an attack at the Somme and form a front with its left flank on the sea and its right on the northern spur of the Maginrt Line. He vividly remembered the long drawn out stalemate that characterized the First World War and greatly feared a repetition. An unsuccessful attack would sap Germany of her strength and could lead to similar results as in 1918.

Though he appeared to endorse the plan, because of his fears, von Rundstedt elected to play a waiting game preferring instead that the Western Allies make the first move. Upon receipt of von Rundstedt's letter in which he expressed his preference for Manstein's plan but adding his own misgivings about an offensive at all, Brauchitsch and Halder suppressed the plan and prevented Hitler from taking courage in von Rundstedt's ambivilent attitude towards an offensive.

Manstein, however, was not to be undone and hoped to reveal his plan to Hitler in the near future.

Between November, 1939 and May, 1940, proposed offensives in the West were postponed eleven times with the usual excuse being bad campaigning weather conditions. On January 9, however, a plane carrying copies of the German attack plan crashed in Belgium. Hitler was furious and ordered a complete revamping of the offensive.

Von Rundstedt was in favor of Manstein's plan being forwarded to the Fuhrer but every attempt to do so was foiled by the Army High Command. For most of late January and early February the German staff reappraised different plans and conducted war games. In a definite move to remove Manstein from the scene, OKH ordered von Rundstedt's Chief-of-Staff to take command of an infantry corps. Fortunately or unfortunately, depending on point of view, the plot backfired for, by giving Manstein a promotion, OKH actually provided the opportunity for his meeting with Hitler.

On February 17, Hitler held a reception for all recently promoted officers. After dinner, a discussion on strategy was conducted providing Manstein with his great opportunity. Hitler, who was himself thinking along the very same lines, was immediately attracted to Manstein's plan and ordered OKH to adopt it.

"Jogged by Rundstedt and reluctantly impressed by the arguments he and his staff had advanced, OKH had ultimately turned the full brainpower of the Zossen* establishment onto their proposals and reduced them to a form which was not only strategically novel but logistically and tactically sound."[5]

The plan called for the use of three Army Groups. Army Group C under von Leeb would play a static role and demonstrate against the Maginot Line thus requiring the French to keep that much vaunted defensive manned at all times. Army Group B under von Bock had as its mission the crushing of the Dutch and Belgium forces and the destruction of their fortifications. Its secondary role was to act as a decoy and entice the crack British and French troops forward into Belgium where they could be crushed by the two converging Army Groups. Von Rundstedt's Army Group A was to play the decisive role. After passing through the heavily wooded Ardennes Forest, it would turn and make directly for the Channel coast, trapping those French and British forces which had charged headlong into Belgium to meet the threat from von Bock. On the surface, the latter was to make the impression that this was indeed the main German thrust.

To accomplish his task, von Rundstedt was alloted forty-five divisions of which seven were armoured and three motorized. The Schwerpunkt was to be accomplished by Kleist's panzer group containing five panzer divisions and the three motorized divisions.

*German Headquarters

Kleist's assignment was to drive through the Ardennes and race to the coast near Abbeville on the mouth of the Somme. The infantry was to follow in it's wake, mopping up by passed pockets of resistance and defending the long and dangerously exposed flank.

The Luftwaffe also was expected to play a vital role and an experienced Air Fleet was assigned to each Army Group. All in all, the German Armed Forces preparing to advance in the west represented one of the most formidable fighting machines in history.

The attack date was finally fixed for May 10, 1940. During preparations for the advance, von Rundstedt was continually bothered by two nagging concerns. His forces must quickly cross the Meuse River and drive rapidly to the channel and his long armoured column must avoid any British or French attacks against it's long exposed flank. In the words of one of the commanders in Army Group A, General Heinz Guderian, speed was of the utmost necessity if success were to be achieved.

By May 12, the impenetrable Ardennes had been penetrated and the Germans stood on the Meuse. Guderian's XIX Panzer Corps, spearheaded by 1st Panzer Division managed to forge a bridgehead over the Meuse at Sedan on May 13. After construction of a pontoon bridge, completed by the early morning of May 14, the drive to the coast resumed in earnest as tanks in large numbers crossed the river obstacle.

As the tanks began crossing the bridge, the

Allies unleashed a desperate air attack. In the midst of this, von Rundstedt turned up and strolled out to join Guderian in the middle of the bridge. While planes strafed and dropped bombs, von Rundstedt casually remarked to Guderian, "Is it always like this here?"

In time, anti-aircraft artillery drove off the Allied air attack while German anti-tank and tank forces pushed back a poorly organized French counterattack which attempted to destroy the German bridgehead. The repulsion of the French attack allowed the Germans to exploit the bridgehead by widening it to fifteen miles deep by thirty miles wide.

As the Panzer divisions left the Meuse behind them, von Rundstedt advanced his headquarters from Koblenz to Charlesville on the Meuse where it was to remain until the conclusion of the critical phase of the campaign. During this battle, von Rundstedt's orthodoxy clearly stood out. The younger Generals, Rommel and Guderian in particular, believed in commanding from the front. Von Rundstedt refuted this theory. Because of the great width of the front with the ever present danger of a French counterattack along the long southern flank, he felt it necessary to remain at his headquarters where he would be able to oversee the total campaign.

Because of his insistance to remain at Charlesville, von Rundstedt took no active part in the daily supervision of the advance to the channel, rather, he found himself more involved in the subordinate movement of Hoth's Panzer Group than with Kleist's which was dashing headlong for the coast. Hoth was in fact encountering stronger resistance because of the very effective demolitions placed on the roads and bridges by the retreating French engineers. Hoth's problem occupied much of Rundstedt's attention.

By May 20, Kleist's panzers had reached the mouth of the Somme at Abbeville and the annihilation of the Allied forces in Belgium looked to be a near, distinct possibility. However, von Rundstedt was not carried away with the elation of the moment. Being a cautious general from the old school, he was not overly optimistic as were his subordinates. Instead, from his position 150 miles behind the line, he remained concerned with the possibilities of French counterattacks against his southern flanks. He refused to be completely at ease until that flank was beefed up with infantry. Fault him for over cautiousness if you will, his fears were not totally without foundation. On May 19, de Gaulle gave the Germans a hard time with a counterattack and two days later, on May 21, the British at Arras did the same. Who was to say what other surprises the Allies had up their sleeves. Had he, however, possessed a direct line into the Headquarters of the Allies, he might have pressed the attack or at least felt more at ease knowing that the Allied plans called for an evacuation.

Compelled by his fears, on May 23, through Kleist, he ordered the armour to halt on the following day until infantry could be brought forward to close the gaps. To Guderian, such a move was an anathema. In his view, he had struggled with faint-hearted leaders and delays throughout most of the campaign and he was concerned that the halt would allow the Allies the needed lee-way to extradite themselves. Guderian's opposition notwithstanding, the drive on the channel ports was halted. On May 24, the order was confirmed by Hitler over the objections of von Brauchitsch. Winston Churchill's memoirs point to von Rundstedt as the one who called the halt. Halder, Chief of the General staff, blames Hitler, basing his conclusion on the theory that Hitler desired the final decisive battle to take place not in Belgium, but in France. Therefore, the Panzers were halted in their tracks.

Though they zealously protested, the Panzer commanders of Army Group A could not persuade von Rundstedt to see it their way. The latter was obsessed with his flanks and the ever present danger of major battles south of the Somme. The spectre of World War I continued to haunt him.

After thirty six hours however, Hitler rescinded the stop order but the damage had already been done. The momentum was forever lost and the delayed advance was slow resulting in a high casualty rate for the Germans. The rest is history, as the British Expeditionary Force and many French troops were extradited via Dunkirk under the eyes of the Germans.

Von Rundstedt was unaffected by the British escape for he was now absorbed in planning his advance south of the Somme. His task for the final battle was the disruption of those French forces east of Paris and a rapid move south to prevent a French withdrawal and linkup with their forces in the south.

The spearhead of von Rundstedt's assault was commanded by Guderian who smashed French resistance with his swift moving southerly attack. By June 17, the new French Government made overtures for an armistice which was concluded on June 22, in the very same railroad car at Compiegne where the armistice ending the First World War was signed. Hitler and Germany had their sweet revenge.

Von Rundstedt's final action in the French campaign found him assisting the Italian Army against the French Alpine forces. He did not relish this particular assignment and objected in harsh language to Halder. Thus ended von Rundstedt's French campaign.

During the campaign, von Rundstedt manifested cool, mature judgement. His conduct can be equated to a character who must know how to manage a team of horses, tightening and loosening the reins when necessary. At times he had to use restraint and at others, he could loosen the manacles.

Berlin revelled in official celebration on July 18. On that day, Hitler promoted nineteen generals to the rank of Colonel-General and nine Colonel-Generals to the rank of Field Marshal, one of whom was Gerd von Rundstedt. Though he should have been proud of that honor, von Rundstedt could not help but feel the integrity and independence of the army gradually slipping away as volleys of honors were lavished on it. More and more, Hitler cemented his control over every aspect of the Army. How could the Army repudiate a leader who so lavishly bestowed such high honors on it's hierarchy? Von Rundstedt was also dismayed with the overabundance of these promotions. During all of the Great War there were only five Field Marshals. Here, after only one year of campaigning with the war still not concluded, Hitler had created nine. To von Rundstedt, the rank seemed devalued.

After the celebrations were over, the new Field Marshal returned to his headquarters in France where he spent the summer of 1940 in relative quiet. His staff, however, was handed the task of planning and executing Operation Sealion, the proposed invasion of England. Von Rundstedt had his doubts that Hitler seriously considered carrying out the invasion and was convinced that Hitler was merely using the threat of invasion to coerce Britain to come to terms with him. Because of this attitude, von Rundstedt did not even visit the units which were to be involved in the operation. For all intents and purposes, Operation Sealion was considered by him to be a bluff.

Britain's intransigence, however, forced Hitler's hand and the Battle of Britain commenced in August. No invasion could be serious-

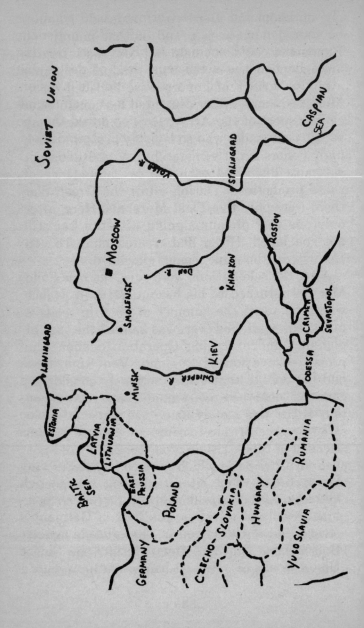

ly contemplated unless Germany held complete domination of the sky. The Luftwaffe, under the command of Reichmarshal Hermann Goering was handed the auspicious task of destroying the Royal Air Force as a prelude to the invasion. As the Luftwaffe's effort faltered, von Rundstedt became more than ever convinced that no cross-channel operation would be attempted in 1940.

As Fall of 1940 turned to the Winter of 1941, von Rundstedt began to suspect that Hitler had other desires than the reduction of Britain. Little by little, von Rundstedt noticed the transfer of commanders and troops from France to the east. Finally, in January, Halder showed up at von Rundstedt's headquarters and revealed the plan for the invasion of Russia, Operation Barbarossa. The Chief-of-Staff desired the keen intelligent appreciation of the Field Marshal and his staff.

Barbarossa called for a three-pronged attack into Russia. The three avenues of advance would be north towards Leningrad, directly eastward towards Moscow, and southward into the Ukraine to the vast industrial and oil regions beyond.

Von Rundstedt was given command of Army Group South which was to advance into the rich Ukraine. Along with his German forces, his command would also include the bulk of Germany's foreign allies who joined in this crusade against Bolshevism. It was estimated that the Soviet Union would be subdued before Autumn with a starting date for the attack in either late April or early May. Wargames held at von Rundstedt's headquarters convinced Halder that the operation was feasible. Feasible or not, however, Hitler was determined to go ahead with the operation.

Throughout the winter, troops were steadily moved to the East. In April, Rundstedt set up his headquarters at Brelau in Silesia.

The original plan called for an attack date in mid-Spring when the ground would be hard enough to support mechanized forces. Unfortunately, events intervened to delay the start of the operation. Up until that time Hitler was able to feel secure that the Balkan states would not cause any trouble while he was involved in his vast campaign in Russia. His ally Italy, however, was experiencing a very difficult time in Greece. On top of this, a pro-German government in Yugoslavia was overthrown in March and an anti-Nazi government was established. This critical situation allowed for the potential of opening up a back door for the British on Germany's southern flank. This determination was reinforced when British troops were sent to Greece in the late winter months of 1941. Hitler realized that before unleashing his blitzkrieg against Russia, the southern flank would have to be made secure. Consequently, operations in the Balkans delayed the beginning of Barbarossa until mid-June.

On June 21, 1941, along a front extending from the Baltic to the Black Sea, the mighty panzers of the German Army blasted their way into the Soviet Union. Initial victories were overwhelming and the elated Germans were convinced that Russia would be defeated in short notice.

Von Rundstedt, however, did not share the elation of the other two Army Group commanders. The original plan for Barbarossa did not give his Army Group the main role. Therefore, his command was not as well equipped with armour as were those of his comrades. Then too, since all the foreign elements were grouped within his command, it lacked cohesiveness.

One other handicap faced von Rundstedt. Though denied the main role in Operation Barbarossa, he was, however, given a number of difficult tasks. First of all, he was directed to drive into the Ukraine with the city of Kiev as his objective. Secondly, he found himself responsible for clearing the coast of the Black Sea as far as Odessa and then make preparations to seize the Crimea. Finally, he was ordered to perform subsidiary tasks beyond the aforementioned prime objectives. Foremost of the latter was an advance to the industrial heartland of Russia, the Donets basin and beyond to the oil regions of Caucasus.

Besides being a military commander with military objectives to be accomplished, von Rundstedt also was forced to be a mediator between the forces of the many nations within his Army Group. The Rumanians and Hungarians were not on speaking terms, yet they had to fight side by side. In short, the command of Army Group South was not the task of "an ordinary soldier."[6]

Not only had von Rundstedt to face all of these problems, but his armies also faced the Soviet South West Front which contained a very large proportion of the Soviet tank units commanded by a highly skilled and determined fighter, General Kirponos.

The first serious Russian counterattack against Army Group South occurred on June 25 and 26. General Kirponos attempted to take Kleist's Panzer Army in the flank and destroy it. Von Rundstedt, the man of experience, correctly diagnosed Kirponos' intentions and lured him into attacking piecemeal, thus denying the Russian the opportunity of launching a concentrated attack. Kleist, whose experience with tanks far exceeded that of his opponent, fell back, drawing the Russians after him. Eventually, the Soviets fell onto a strong German defensive screen of the famours 88mm anti-aircraft/anti-tank guns which hastily scattered and destroyed all Soviet tanks within range.

Following this defeat, Kirponos withdrew his Fifth Army into the Pripet Marshes, a vast area of wet, marshy, swamp land. Von Rundstedt remembered this region well from his experiences during the First World War and refused to allow his formations to follow in the Soviet wake. Three weeks later, however, Kirponos' Fifth Army emerged from the marshes for another crack at Army Group South. Once again the Russian commander desired to attack the Germans in the flank but this time his plans were a bit more ambitious. He wished his Fifth Army to attack near Zhitomir, drive through the German flank, and join hands near Berdichev with the Soviet Sixth Army which was to attack northwards. The outnumbered Germans once more skillfully outfought the Russians in a battle that lasted several days and saw the virtual destruction of the Russian mechanized corps. Again, the Fifth Army fled to the safety of the Pripet Marshes, exhausted and with its fighting ability reduced to nil.

Kiev now fully began to preoccupy von Rundstedt's thoughts. The city stood within but a day's march of his most forward forces. However, he felt that to commit his forces to it would be a strategical error, for the city had a large garrison situated behind formidable defenses. A pitched battle there would mean heavy street fighting and sap the German strength, particularly that of the panzers which were more suited to the open terrain where they could more rapidly thrust into the enemy defenses. Tying them down in street fighting could prove disastrous.

Though he halted his drive on Kiev in mid-July, it did not necessarily mean that his Army Group was to be passive. He recognized the possibility of exploiting a great victory around the city of Uman, well south of Kiev. There, a large quantity of Soviet forces were concentrated and he saw an excellent opportunity of achieving an encirclement of the enemy formations in that vicinity.

By August 2, the encirclement became a reality and the Soviet formations were cut off but continued to fight until August 8. On that date, 100,000 Russian survivors began their long march off to prisoner of war camps. Though a paltry sum in comparison to the encirclement battles accomplished by Army Groups North and Center, it was von Rundstedt's first major encirclement victory in the Russian campaign.

Kiev now became von Rundstedt's primary objective but in order to obtain it, he reasoned that armour from Army Group Center would have to be loaned to his command. This opened up one of the most controversial debates of the entire Eastern Front, the decision of which many historians to this day blame as the cause of the German failure to achieve total victory in 1941. The crux of the matter rested on the matter of what constituted the primary objective of Operation Barbarossa.

Guderian and Bock, commander of Army Group Center, felt that the armour concentration should be continued towards Moscow which was only 200 miles from the point of the German advance. Hitler, however, fearful that an advance too deep in the center without a corresponding advance in the north and south could expose his central forces to attack from both flanks. For all his boldness, Hitler was not bold enough to risk the full implication of the blitzkrieg theory. Rather, he felt that for security purposes, all three advances should be abreast. In addition, economics were beginning to take hold of Hitler. He desired the possession of the valuable lands of the Ukraine and the industrial region of the Donets Basin. Thus, on July 19, he issued a new Fuhrer Directive which altered the strategic aim of Barbarossa. This new directive exposed a great discrepancy in the reasoning between Hitler and his generals. The military men always felt that the aim of the campaign was the destruction of the Russian Army. But the Fuhrer emphasized that the acquisition of 'living space' was the primary objective. Consequently, in Fuhrer order No. 33, he stripped von Bock of his armour, sending Hoth's Panzer Army northward to assist von Leeb's Army Group North with the capture of Leningrad, and Guderian's 2nd Panzer Army south to help Kleist in the encirclement of Kiev with the ultimate objective of acquiring the breadbasket of Russia as living space for the Reich.

Guderian was definitely not in favor of this change of direction and attempted to use all his influence to convince Hitler not to send him south. He even went so far as to gain an audience with Hitler personally but he acquiesced in the latter's presence.

By September 16, the leading elements of Guderian's Panzer Army linked up with Kleist's east of Kiev. In doing so, the two Panzer Armies managed to trap over half a million Soviet soldiers in the Kiev pocket. Fighting within the pocket was desperate but by September 26, it was all over. By this time however, von Rundstedt was pushing his other forces forward to lay siege to Odessa while the Eleventh Army, under his former Chief-of-Staff, von Manstein, was crossing the Dniepr River as far as the entrance to the Crimea.

No sooner was von Rundstedt able to push forward with these ambitious endeavors when his ability to achieve them was stifled by the denuding of the strength of his Army Group. After the conclusion of the battles around Kiev, he was ordered to return a number of his forces to Army Group Center. Those forces remaining were suffering from exhaustion after three solid months of fighting and needed to pause to catch their breath. Moreover, the Fall weather was approaching promising to bring with it mud and the dreaded cold.

Meanwhile, Kleist's Panzer Army continued its advance towards Rostov until muddy roads became impassable and brought the advance to a standstill on October 14. Von Rundstedt now attempted an advance into the Don Bend. Northwest of Rostov, at Kahrkov, the Germans inflicted heavy losses on the Russians causing them to fall back behind the Donets with von Reichenau's Sixth Army in hot pursuit.

On November 5, Kleist's forces drove the Soviet Ninth Army twenty miles back from the Mius River and levered the enemy's Fifty-Sixth Army out of its position covering Rostov.

The battle for Rostov had already commenced on November 2, and ended in a Pyrrhic victory for the Germans. The Russians, under one of their more able commanders, Timoshenko, launched a series of fierce counterattacks with fresh troops and threatened the rear of the German position at Rostov and, on November 28, the city was abandoned by the Germans who fell back on the Mius.

Shortly thereafter, the boom was lowered on von Rundstedt. On the evening of November 30, he received word from Brauchitsch that Hitler had forbidden any withdrawal whatsoever. The campaign had already been a terrible strain on his health which had deteriorated greatly during the last month causing him to suffer a mild heart-attack. Upon receipt of the no withdrawal order, he asked to be relieved of his command.

Von Reichenau, an ardent Nazi and commander of the Sixth Army, was appointed to replace von Rundstedt as commander of Army Group South. Ironically, the new commander found himself compelled to carry out the very same order for which von Rundstedt had been called on the carpet.

Hitler personally travelled to Poltava, southwest of Kharkov, on December 3 to investigate the situation. He requested that von Rundstedt be brought before him and openly demonstrated warm friendship and understanding for the plight of the aging Field Marshal. Von Manstein stated that:

"Hitler always had a soft spot for von Rundstedt."[6]

The Fuhrer begged von Rundstedt to accept the fact that it was merely a misunderstanding that had occurred between them and that it was only the poor health of the Field Marshal that prevented him from being reassigned immediately.

Both parted on friendly terms which is more than could be said for the other two Army Group Commanders (Leeb and Bock), two Panzer Army Commanders (Guderian and Hoeppner), thirty-five Corps or Divisional commanders, and General Brauchitsch, the Commander-in-Chief of the Army. All were relieved from duty.

Von Rundstedt went home on sick leave to his home at Kassel but was told by Hitler to remain at his disposal.

In March, 1942, after three months of recuperation, von Rundstedt was summoned by Hitler to assume the position of Commander-in-Chief West. There he found that his new position was more than just a military one as subordinate to him were the military governors of occupied France and Belgium. He was also required to act as intermediary between Hitler and the head of the Vichy French Government, Marshal Petain. Furthermore, he found himself commanding all military units in his zone, including air and naval units, which were all answerable to his orders.

In time, von Rundstedt was to find that his power was not as extensive as he had originally thought it to be. He found that the two military governors were his subordinates for limited purposes only as they dealt for the most part directly with OKW. The Luftwaffe and the Kreigsmarine were required to accept his orders only if they concerned the safety of the coasts.

As Commander-in-Chief West, his primary concern was the preparation of his forces and defenses for an eventual invasion by the western Allies. Where and when the attack would come provided the greatest puzzle for his staff. Von Rundstedt determined that for the ultimate security of the lengthy coastal sector, fixed formations were not the answer for the repulsion of an invasion. Rather, he exhorted the need for the formation of an armoured reserve which could be rapidly deployed at any danger spot. This he felt was the key to stopping the Allies. Hitler, however, favored fixed fortifications.

Von Rundstedt pointed out the need for additional personnel to protect the vast seacoast but his requests were not well received by Hitler who at this time was fully committed to a life and death struggle in the east. Nonetheless, in November, 1943, the Fuhrer issued a new Fuhrer Directive (No. 51) in which he laid down the principles on how the west would be defended. The first point of the directive called for reinforcements, particularly of the armoured formations. The next point stated that the Allied invasion force must be counterattacked immediately when it appeared and thrown back into the sea. The directive did not, however, state who would control the reserve and where it would be positioned.

In November, 1943, a new actor appeared on

the stage of von Rundstedt's command. Field Marshal Erwin Rommel, the famed Desert Fox, was appointed by Hitler to be Inspector of Coastal Fortifications. Field Marshal Keitel, Chief of OKW, arrived at von Rundstedt's headquarters before the arrival of Rommel in order to explain the latter's functions. Von Rundstedt was informed that Rommel would come under his command for tactical purposes in the event of an emergency. The former had originally feared that conflict would arise between he and his ambitious subordinate and these fears were not laid to rest even with Keitel's assurances.

When Rommel arrived, Keitel invited both Field Marshals to a joint discussion on their responsibilities. The meeting was cordial and understanding was reached between the two. Rommel accepted a command structure which von Rundstedt subsequently endorsed and forwarded to Hitler. Rommel's Army Group B would be incorporated into the command structure immediately below von Rundstedt but above the armies. Included in Army Group B were Seventh and Fifteenth Armies in the Normandy and Pas de Calais areas. Hitler accepted this arrangment and issued orders for its implementation on December 31, 1943.

Early in January, General Alfred Jodl, Chief Operations Officer at OKW made an inspection tour of the western coasts. The significant part of this tour was the concern that OKW expressed for the Western Front. In a peculiar command arrangement, OKH held command responsibility for the Eastern Theatre while OKW was responsible for all other fronts.

Rommel was familiar with the way OKW operated since his former command in North Africa had been under the tactical command of this office. Thus, he hoped to have some advantage in case a tug of war developed between he and von Rundstedt, especially in the debate that now arose between them over deployment of the armoured reserve.

Rommel, who had the benefit of first hand experience with the destructive power of allied airpower, argued that the armoured divisions should be situated as close as possible to the threatened beaches so that they could intervene at the earliest possible stage of the allied landing. Early intervention would allow the Germans to throw the Allies back into the sea before they could establish a firm toehold on the shore and bring up their weapons. Should the Allies be allowed to establish a beachhead, Rommel went on, it would be most difficult, if not impossible, to move the armoured units by day under the eye of the allied airforces who would then be able to wreak havoc with communications and troop movements.

Von Rundstedt advocated that the last remaining chance lay in a mobile defense and that the enemy could be defeated in the heart of France by superior strategy and by inflicting such heavy losses on them that they would be ready for a compromise peace.

The debate went on throughout the Spring of

1944. Finally, von Rundstedt personally travelled to Berchtesgarten in April to visit Hitler and urge adoption of his plan. Hitler appeared to give his nominal agreement but the result was not completely to von Rundstedt's liking. Yes, a central reserve was formed; but von Rundstedt would not be allowed to order it about without the express permission of Hitler.

As April turned to May, both commanders were certain that the invasion would be soon. The big question plaguing Hitler and the German High Command was not only when would the invasion come, but where. Through various deceptive operations, the Allies had so thoroughly deceived the Germans that the latter were groping in the dark. Hitler himself was convinced that the invasion would take place in the Pas de Calais area. The Allies fed Hitler's premonitions by presenting irrefutable evidence that the Pas de Calais was most certainly the logical place for invasion. Any other invasion would be merely a diversion aimed at dissipating German strength at the main invasion site. Von Rundstedt's attention, however, was focused on Normandy.

The Germans knew that conditions ideal for an invasion would exist between June 4 and 7th. Bad weather, however, relaxed their fear of an Allied assault. Consequently, Rommel left his headquarters on June 5 to spend time with his wife on her birthday. Late that night, word reached von Rundstedt's staff of Allied paratroop landings. Von Rundstedt's staff took the necessary precautionary measures, warning the coastal defenses to be alert to the possibility of an invasion. When von Rundstedt received firm confirmation of the strength and whereabouts of the airborne landings, he realized that he would have to move his panzer divisions quickly into place.

Though the Allies landed successfully on June 6, 1944, thanks to the quick action of von Rundstedt and the stiff opposition of the German troops, they were denied the objective that they had set for themselves for the first evening; a continuous bridgehead. Von Rundstedt then realized that only a counterattack of great strength launched quickly would deny the Allies the opportunity of consolidating their bridgehead.

The armour which von Rundstedt so desperately required was then at the Pas de Calais waiting for the 'real invasion.' Thanks to Allied deception, Hitler was convinced that the Normandy landings were merely a feint and that the real invasion would soon follow. Therefore, he refused to free the desperately needed Panzers for use in Normandy. Von Rundstedt, although he openly admitted that the Allies had the capability of landing at a number of places, considered Normandy to be the real invasion point. Had Hitler acquiesced, the outcome of the Normandy landings might have been disastrous for the Allies.

On June 10, and again the following day, von Rundstedt requested OKW to arrange a personal interview with Hitler for him. What he desired foremost was freedom of maneuver for without it, his hands would be tied. The Allies were busily consolidating their bridgehead and accomplished this on June 12. Therefore, von Rundstedt was convinced that without the ability to maneuver freely, the German Army in Normandy was doomed to defeat. With that freedom, he would be able to conduct strategic withdrawals to the West Wall with the minimum of casualties. Once behind these defenses, he could then prepare for a decisive battle.

The desired meeting took place on June 17. Von Rundstedt, with his traditional General Staff outlook, came prepared to wrest from Hitler a broad directive granting him full operational control of the campaign. Instead, the Fuhrer spoke for four hours on the new secret weapons which were eventually to bring ultimate victory to Germany. The conference ended without anything concrete being settled.

For the next two weeks, the German situation in Normandy continued to deteriorate at an alarming rate. The Allies successfully managed to enlarge their foothold on the continent despite the fact that the Germans fought tooth and nail and made the Allies pay dearly for every inch of ground gained.

Hitler's flunky, Field Marshal Keitel, telephoned von Rundstedt nightly to obtain the current situational reports. On July 1, von Rundstedt reported that four SS Panzer divisions facing the British had failed to stop the British advance. Keitel frantically cried, "What shall we do?" "Make peace you fools"[7] was von Rundstedt's curt reply. Keitel reported the conversation immediately to Hitler who decided that the time had come for the 'old man' to be relieved. Field Marshal Gunther von Kluge, a Hitler favorite, was selected as the replacement.

Von Rundstedt received the news of his dismissal on July 2. Once again, the pretext used by Hitler was the health of the aging Field Marshal. The next day, a member of Hitler's staff arrived at von Rundstedt's headquarters with a personal letter of regret from Hitler who nevertheless, awarded von Rundstedt the Oak Leaves to the Knight's Cross. Although he was once again unemployed, Hitler continued to think kindly of him. On July 6, he left Paris and for the third time, set off into retirement.

Because of von Rundstedt's apolitical beliefs, he was never approached by the conspirators who were making plans to assassinate Hitler. On July 20, the attempt on Hitler's life was unsuccessfully made by a small band of military figures. The attempt to seize the reins of government likewise failed. Because of his unblemished reputation and Hitler's paranoia towards the military, the German leader turned once more to the one man whom he could trust, Field Marshal von Rundstedt.

With the failure of the coup d' etat, Hitler wreaked terrible retribution against the military and requested von Rundstedt to sit on a Court of Honor which had the distasteful duty of expelling the conspirators from the military so that these officers could be turned over to the People's Court to be tried as civilians for treason.

Though this duty must have been highly distasteful to him, as a soldier von Rundstedt knew he must do his duty. He performed it believing that once a soldier involves himself in political intrigue, he surrenders his status as a solider. Once more, the traditional teachings of the General Staff became evident.

Meanwhile, the Allied breakout from Normandy and the headlong retreat of the Wermacht across France with the subsequent demoralization of the German troops, exposed the need for a stabilizing influence to be dispatched to France with all haste. On September 5, the old Field Marshal once again was called to resume command in the west.

The German retreat to their fixed defenses coupled with Allied overextension caused the front to stabilize temporarily in the Autumn. The skillfully conducted defensive battles for Aachen and the Ruhr attested to von Rundstedt's ability and General Staff training.

While von Rundstedt was concentrating on these Autumn battles, the fertile mind of Hitler was concocting a plan that would distract the Field Marshal from the task at hand. Hitler was contemplating an operation that was designed to turn the tide in the West.

Hitler's 'Last Gamble' was designed to follow the path of his great victory of 1940 but the ultimate objective was changed. This time it was to be Antwerp. As the Eastern front stabilized with the onset of Winter, Hitler felt that an all out attack in the West could knock out the Western Allies, split them in two, and force them to sue for peace. Then, with this accomplished, Germany could devote her full attention to the defeat of the Russians.

On October 24, von Rundstedt was familiarized with the details of Hitler's master plan and took an immediate dislike to it. He was convinced that defeat was imminent and that instead of squandering the last German strength in an offensive doomed to failure, this strength should be husbanded and used to fight defensively from within the German borders.

Hitler, however, refused to be swayed and ordered the offensive to commence as planned and von Rundstedt, as a loyal soldier, was designated to command it whether he liked it or not. Although tactical command rested with the two Army Commanders, (Dietrich and Maunteuffel) under the supervision of Rommel's successor in command of Army Group B, Field Marshal Walther Model, the offensive was not only known as the Battle of the Bulge, but the Allies also referred to it as the von Rundstedt offensive when in fact he played a very small role in the entire affair.

Von Rundstedt attempted one last time to change Hitler's mind. Accepting the fact that Hitler would have his offensive, he endeavored to persuade the Fuhrer to lessen the extent of the offensive. This modified plan, known as the small solution, would set as its goal Liege, an American supply base. To seek a penetration as far as Antwerp was madness. Under von Rundstedt's proposal, the Germans would still break out of the Ardennes but move only as far as was necessary to inflict serious damage. By attacking Liege, the Allied advance could be slowed and time bought for the beleaguered German Army. Hitler refused to modify the plan stating that the original plan, or large solution, with Antwerp as the ultimate objective, would go ahead as originally planned.

Sadly for von Rundstedt, he was proved totally correct and the grandiose plans of Adolf Hitler resulted in a bitter defeat for the Wermacht in the West. Although the Germans had managed to give the Americans a severe mauling, by Christmas it was clear that Germany's last offensive had failed miserably.

Von Rundstedt was now the only stabilizing influence remaining on the collapsed Western front. All his suggestions, however, were usually rejected as the demented dictator could no longer logically accept the truth.

On March 7, 1945, the Americans captured an intact bridge over the Rhine River at Remagen. Hitler was furious, ranting and raving and seeking scapegoats to satisfy his ravings. Von Rundstedt was summoned to Fuhrer headquarters on March 9. When he was ushered into Hitler's presence, there was no rage on the part of the demented leader, rather, the presence of the venerable Field Marshal seemed to exert a settling influence on the Fuhrer. He actually thanked the old soldier for his many years of faithful service and presented him with the Swords to the Knight's Cross. Following this brief ceremony, von Rundstedt left. It was the last time they ever saw each other.

For the fourth and final time, von Rundstedt went into retirement at Bad Tolz. There he was taken prisoner by the Americans in May. After his capture, he would spend over three years in prison, most of the time in England. To the International Military Tribunal at Nuremberg he presented evidence which made a considerable impression on those present. He was never accused of war crimes, nor was he ever arraigned even though he took part in almost every major campaign. In 1953, in his seventy eighth year, Gerd von Rundstedt died.

How can this man be evaluated? John Keegan put it so aptly:

"He had set an example of military virtue, he stood instantly revealed as that rarest sort of general, a soldier's soldier. He was not perhaps a great captain, but he was a man of intelligence and honour. And he was the last of that admirable military type: The Prussian Great General Staff Officer.[8]

Von Rundstedt truly was, as Liddell-Hart described him, "a gentleman to the core." Though he has stated that he was not a great captain, he was however, a true leader. He inspired his men, he instilled a sense of confidence on his subordinates and even on Hitler himself. The greatest blot against this man was that he acquiesced to the mad ravings of the Corporal turned Dictator. It appears that he played along with Hitler, doing his bidding, without grasping the larger picture or seeing the deeper implication of his actions. His service on the Court of Honor also detracts from his personality and bears witness to his total collusion with the Nazis. An oath, however, was something to be taken quite seriously by him and he never failed to live up to it. In fact, oath, honor, loyalty, was bread and butter to this aristocratic Prussian. Rather than being condemned, he should be understood, which is not an easy task. General Gunther Blumentritt, his operations officer during the Polish and French campaigns, then his Chief-of-Staff during his time as Commander-in-Chief, West, said that "Von Rundstedt was a comparatively complex character, not easy to understand . . . he strove in vain for poise and harmony of mind."

Honor and loyalty were his paths to the peace of mind. It was his heritage. By being honorable, by his loyalty to his oath, he found peace of mind even if it meant following the dictates of a dishonorable government.

Chapter 3

Military leaders are frequently among the most famous and respected men of their age, however distasteful war itself may be. A general, uniting within himself a dynamic personality and an above average intelligence tempered by common sense, can rightfully expect fame to come to him. Although unable to survive WW II, Field Marshal Erwin W. Rommel was one of those dynamic personalities who, in his lifetime, achieved unprecedented notoriety. Perhaps the tremendous achievements in the field of communications during the twentieth century made the heights of fame that much easier to scale. However, as we move further away from the Second World War, future military scholars will undoubtedly rate Rommel as one of the finest military tacticians of WW II.

Recent scholarship has unfolded many long hidden secrets of WWII, among which is the secret of Ultra. Ultra is the name given to the top grade intercepted German signals which, thanks to the efforts of Polish, French and British cryptographers were made available to the Allied commanders. These intercepted signals gave the Allies an open channel into the deep secrets of German Military Intelligence.

In evaluating Rommel, we must therefore retain knowledge of this handicap; every message he forwarded to the German High Command and the Commando Supremo in Rome was simultaneously read by his opponents. In many instances, even before the intended recipient had access to the message. Though the Germans never caught on to the fact that their supposedly unbreakable Enigma cipher was indeed broken, this did not mean that Rommel had no secret intelligence of his own. Again, unfolded secrets have shown to us that Rommel too was reading ciphers; those of the American Military Attache in Cairo, Col. Fellers, who used the supposedly safe "Black Code" when transmitting messages to Washington. Not until July of 1942 was it realized that the "Black Code" cipher was compromised. Rommel called these cipher extracts his "Little Fellows," in honor of Col. Fellers. In addition, Rommel's intelligence crew tapped into the British wireless conversations which surprisingly enough, had very lax security. All in all, when appraising Rommel, as we intend to do within this chapter, it is absolutely essential that we bear in mind the role of secret intelligence.

Rommel viewed the desert of North Africa for the first time in February, 1941. The British command in the Middle East were the recipients of an intelligence signal announcing the arrival at Tripoli of the leading elements of a German Motorized Division. The British intelligence section assessed the German commander as a relatively unknown, with no significant record of accomplishment and continued on to speculate about the unfeasibility of an early Axis offensive. However, the British were due to learn the hard way, for already, before he ever came to the shores of North Africa, Erwin Rommel had proven himself an accomplished leader.

During WW I, Rommel had been a relatively junior officer, but one who demonstrated his skill as a leader during the many battles against the Italians. Ironically, it was these former foes, the Italians, who he would now lead with unparalleled brilliance. For his WW I exploits, he was awarded the coveted "Pour le Merite" (the Blue Max), Germany's highest decoration for valor. The talent demonstrated during this conflict brought him to the attention of the senior officers of the army, paving his way for selection to the small cadre of officers allotted to Germany under the harsh terms of the Treaty of Versailles.

The post-war years found Rommel holding the usual variety of staff positions before being posted to the War College, in the 1930's, as an instructor of infantry tactics. It was during this time that Rommel authored a book on the subject that he found himself teaching. Adolf Hitler, a voracious reader of military textbooks, poured over Rommel's book and was immediately impressed. When Germany began to prepare for the march into Czechoslovakia, the Nazi leader ordered that Rommel be assigned to command his personal bodyguard. After the bloodless victory over the unfortunate Czechs, Rommel was promoted to Major General while retaining his position as head of Hitler's bodyguard for the forthcoming Polish campaign.

The lightning campaign against Poland was cause for jubilation at Hitler's headquarters. The German leader lavished rewards upon his military leaders and field commanders. Rommel was not overlooked, for by now, he had become a favorite at court. When queried about the type of command he next desired, the future Field Marshal did not hesitate to request command of a Panzer Division. Hitler, almost immediately, confirmed Rommel's appointment as commander of the 7th Panzer Division, succeeding General Stumme.

In mid-February, 1940, Rommel assumed his new command on the Western Front. The 7th Panzer Division was one of two comprising General Hoth's XV Panzer Corps in General von Kleist's Panzer Group. All were under the overall command of General Gerd von Rundstedt, commander of Army Group A and the senior general of the German Army. During the period that came to be known as the "Phoney War," Rommel used the time to study the teachings of Liddel-Hart and Fuller regarding the role of tanks in modern warfare. He was already acquainted with General Heinz Guderian's tactics, which he was able to observe first-hand during the Polish campaign. Undoubtedly, this helped form the brilliant tank theories that would come to make Rommel's name a household word.

Responsible for the right wing of Hoth's advance, which itself constituted the extreme northerly section of Panzer Group Kleist, the 7th Panzer Division crossed the Belgian frontier on May 10, 1940. Within three days, leading elements of his division, Rommel himself at the front, were already on the Meuse River where Rommel personally assisted in building a bridge over the water obstacle. Though slightly wounded the next day by French anti-tank fire, Rommel moved steadily forward, practicing the doctrine that to be successful, a Panzer Division must be led from the front and should be constantly on the move, a belief that he retained for the balance of his illustrious career.

By May 16, he had broken through the Allied defenses and was headed on a dash for the Channel coast. The 7th Panzer drove relentlessly on, even rolling forward at night to reduce casualties. So rapid was their advance that the French citizenry, refusing to accept the presence of Germans so far in the rear of what was supposed to be the front, hailed Rommel's troops as saviors instead of conquerors. However, once the German insignia on the side of Rommel's tanks became recognizable, disillusionment followed rapidly.

On May 20, Rommel was near Arras where he made plans for a final thrust to the coast. But, so swift was his advance, that he had outrun his neighbor to the south, the 5th Panzer Division. Thus, an opportunity for blunting the German spearhead presented itself to the British who sent forward a concentrated counterattack aimed at the destruction of the 7th Panzer. Despite heavy losses, Rommel managed to stave off destruction by using his 88 millimeter anti-aircraft guns in an anti-tank role. He was further able to summon Stuka dive bombers from near-by fields, which supplied instant support by virtue of the Luftwaffe's total command of the skies after their spectacular victory over the British and French Air Forces.

Regrouping after his initial set back, Rommel was ordered by Hoth on June 6, to set off for the coast and prevent the British from evacuating the continent in a maneuver which had already begun. By June 9, Rommel had reached the Seine near Rouen and continued across the river to arrive at St. Valery on the coast during the day of June 11. The following day, he stormed that port and managed to capture almost the entire 51st Highland Division along with its commander, General Fortune. From St. Valery, the 7th Panzer pressed on along the Cherbourg Peninsula and by June 19, the port of Cherbourg itself was in German hands along with many senior British and French generals and admirals. Except for a relatively unopposed drive southward along the French Coast, the French campaign was now over for Rommel and his men. Dreary, restless days of occupation duty now set in. Rommel however used the time judiciously studying the French language, culture and customs.

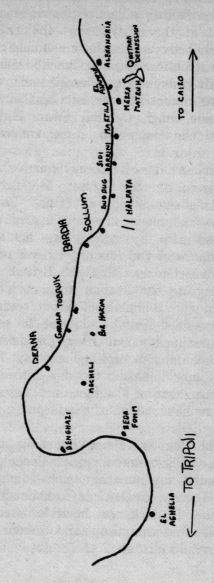

Early in 1941, Hitler decided to send aid to his failing Italian allies whose reversals in North Africa had visibly upset the Fuhrer. Hitler, pleased that Rommel's success more than justified his confidence, quickly selected the latter to command the expedition, over the emphatic objections of the Chief of the German General Staff, General Franz Halder. Troops were then assembled to prepare for the trip to North Africa.

Within days of Rommel's arrival, the leading elements of the German 5th Light Division began disembarking at Tripoli. Rommel meanwhile had made excellent use of the time afforded him by conducting an aerial reconnaissance of the forward British positions. His appreciation was that the British were not as strong as the Italian reports indicated. Immediately, Rommel set about reorganizing the demoralized Italians while at the same time acculturating his own troops for life in the desert. Desert life! How unlike Germany. The heat, the early morning cold, the dry barren wastelands, not to mention the incessant desert flies. One author has written of the flies:

"The foul and dismaying thing about the flies was their oneness. None was separate from its fellows any more than the wave is separate from the ocean, the tentacle from the octopus. As one fly, one dark and horrible force guided by one mind, ubiquitous and immensely powerful, they addressed themselves to the one task, which was to destroy us body and soul. It was useless to kill them, for they despised death and made no attempt to avoid it. They existed only in the common will, and to weaken that we should have had to destroy countless millions of them. None the less, we killed them unceasingly. We killed them singly and in detachments with fly swats and the dead lay so thick in our lorries that we had to sweep them out several times a day. We set ingenious traps for them and they filled the traps, the living feasting ghoulishly on the dead. We slew them in mounds with our bare hands until the crunch of minute frames and the squash of microscopic viscera, felt rather than heard, became a nightmare. Flies are attracted by any light surface and our towels and the sun bleached canopies of our lorries speckled as with black confetti. Flies crave moisture and you knew from watching your friends and the knowledge was disproportionately humiliating and disgusting ... and when you shut your eyes, flies tried to open them, mad for the delectable fluid.

We couldn't always be killing them but we had to keep brushing them away, otherwise even breathing would have been difficult. Our arms ached from the exercise, but still they fastened on our food and accompanied it into our mouths and down our throats, scorning death when there was an advantage to be gained. They drowned themselves in our tea and soup!"[1]

And so the Germans settled into desert life with its multitude of discomforts.

Rommel however, was not one to stand idly by and let opportunity pass, for he was anxious to get his forces moving, the desert discomforts notwithstanding.

In actuality, the British defenses were weaker than even Rommel dared hope. Many of the front line troops had been pulled out and dispatched to Greece in an abortive attempt to salvage the increasingly critical situation there. Others had been recalled to Cairo for rest and reorganization including Lt. General Sir Richard O'Connor, the conquering hero and commander of the British desert fighting forces. He was in Cairo and in his place came General Philip Neame, a man devoid of desert experience and totally lacking in knowledge of armoured warfare. Neame would prove to be no match for the wily and clever Rommel.

After a month of ineffectual attacks which were designed to probe the British defenses, Rommel launched a full scale assault on the night of March 31, 1941 contrary to orders from Berlin not to attack until the arrival of the 15th Panzer division, due to arrive early in May.

Rommel however, was not a commander to let opportunity pass, for he recognized the weakness of his opponent and was eager to exploit it.

Neame had meanwhile decided to withdraw his leading elements to a firmer base near Mersa el Brega. Rommel's attack hit the British when their position was most vulnerable; while they were in the process of moving up to these positions. The British line was swiftly breached at Mersa el Brega which fell on the first day. After four days of continued advance, Benghazi fell, and with it tons of badly needed supplies that the British failed to destroy in their haste to evacuate that city.

Now, in a near duplication of O'Connor's earlier marvelous effort, Rommel sent the Italians racing along the coastal roads towards Brace while he personally led the 5th Light off in a march across the desert towards the British position at Mechili. Rommel, drawing his own conclusions regarding the use of armour in the desert, recognized its ability to operate in this terrain and was determined to grasp the potential rewards that could be reaped.

Neame meanwhile, had requested that O'Connor come up from Cairo to serve in an advisory capacity. The British commander had clearly sacrificed the initiative and the situation was now approaching the critical stage. O'Connor wasted no time flying in from Cairo, hoping to assist Neame in stablizing the front. Unfortunately for the British, during the night of April 6, the two generals were touring the front in their staff car when they blundered into the leading elements of the German 5th Light Division and were taken prisoner. Thus, in one fell swoop, Rommel managed to capture not only the actual commander of the British forces opposing him, but the former commander and architect of the earlier spectacular British victories over the Italians as well. Another senior commander in the Mechili area, General Gambier-Parry was shortly to follow Neame and O'Connor into captivity. With their only knowledgeable desert tactician now a prisoner, the British position rapidly became untenable.

Rommel meanwhile, sensing the initiative was now in his hands, wasted little time in pressing on towards Tobruk. Field Marshall Sir Archibald Wavell, the British Commander-in-Chief, Middle East, finding command suddenly resting on his shoulders, correctly deduced that Tobruk would be the next objective of Rommel. Without delay, he rushed reinforcements to this important port realizing what the consequences would be should Tobruk fall into Axis hands.

Rommel demonstrated briefly against the Tobruk defenses but swiftly perceived that his unsupported and undermanned troops would find it impossible to storm a heavily fortified position. Reluctantly, he pushed on towards the Egyptian border and by April 30, both Bardia and Sollum had fallen to his victorious troops. In less than six weeks, the fruits of O'Connor's brilliant Cyrenician campaign had been nullified.

Rommel now began the task of laying siege to Tobruk. With the Luftwaffe pounding the British positions daily, Rommel probed for weaknesses in the defenses with his troops. The Australians within the city grimly, and with dedicated determination, refused to yield despite heavy losses. A half hearted British counteroffensive, Operation Brevity, was launched by Wavell on May 15, in an effort to relieve the beleaguered Australians, but it was quickly beaten off and the siege of Tobruk continued.

Rommel's offensive had now run its course. Outrunning his supplies, he was forced to pause and regroup. In addition, these supply lines stretched for hundreds of miles across a desert dominated by the British Desert Air Force whose constant harrassment became a cause of great concern and a thorn in Rommel's side.

However, the opposite was true for the British; troops began streaming back to North Africa after the debacle in Greece. Churchill, realizing that North Africa was now the only theatre available to strike a blow at the Axis, began dispatching additional men and material to Wavell. Furthermore, through Ultra, the British Prime Minister was aware of the Axis' critical supply position and began pressuring Wavell into striking immediately. The result was the ill-fated Operation Battleaxe, aimed at the destruction of Rommel and the relief of Tobruk.

On June 15, Battleaxe was launched towards Tobruk. Though initially taken back by the strength of the British attack, Rommel wasted little time in locating the weak points, which were many, and made the most of the opportunities afforded to him because of the hasty way in which the British organized their offensive. First, the British placed their armour in scattered groups to support the assaulting infantry, while Rommel, with his customary skillful use of tanks, concentrated his armour and smashed each British unit as it appeared in front of him. Secondly, the British charged with their tanks in a manner strangely reminiscent of the ancient cavalry charges. Rommel, luring the British armour just were he wanted it, destroyed them with his dug in 88's (that famous German anti-aircraft gun that was subsequently used extensively as an anti-tank gun). Two days after its beginning, Battleaxe had shot its bolt and Wavell wisely but reluctantly recalled his troops to their jumping off position and cancelling Battleaxe, which had proved a costly failure.

A command crisis finally came to a head among the British forces. Churchill and Wavell never had been able to see things in the same light. This personality conflict, coupled with the complete failure of the ill-fated Battleaxe, resulted in Wavell, a worn out and much dispirited man, being sent off to India. In his place came Sir Claude Auchinleck, fresh from that same theatre. On him were pinned the hopes of the British forces. In effect, Auchinleck and Wavell had virtually swapped commands.

Although Auchinleck would subsequently prove to be one of England's most outstanding commanders of the war, a fact which Rommel was to heartily endorse, he was shortly after his arrival to make some severe errors in judgement. The first order of business was to select someone to be the new commander of the British desert forces and Auchinleck tabbed General Sir Alan Cunningham. On the surface, it appeared to have been a wise choice since Cunningham's record was impressive, having conducted a faultless campaign during the victory over the Italians in Abyssinia. However, beneath the surface, there existed fatal flaws.

Cunningham was devoid of experience with large armoured formations; he was totally unfamiliar with conditions in the desert, and most important, he was physically and mentally exhausted from his months of campaigning in the interior. It was an ominous beginning as the British began preparing, for better or for worse, a relief campaign aimed at driving the Axis out of Africa and lifting the siege of Tobruk.

Although the flow of British reinforcements continued, Rommel too found himself reinforced. The 15th Panzer Division had finally joined him on the Egyptian frontier. In addition, the 5th Light Division had been strengthened and rechristened the 21st Panzer Division. Generals Neuman-Silkow and von Ravenstein respectively were the commanders and considered to be very aggressive. General Ludwig Cruewell also arrived in the desert at this point, to take command of these two divisions, now combined into a command designated the Deutches Afrika Korps. Rommel meanwhile, had been promoted to command of Panzerarmee Afrika, with the rank of General der Panzertruppen. His new command consisted of the Afrika Korps and the Italian formations. The Italians also reinforced their formations and contributed a tank division copied from the Germans, naming this division the Ariete. This division would later demonstrate that they were indeed brave soldiers and did much to refute the abuse and contempt heaped upon the Italians as fighters.

At this point, Rommel was not burdened with interference from home as were the British commanders. Hitler's focus was on Russia so he allowed himself to be convinced by his military advisors in particular Col. General Franz Halder, Chief of the German General Staff and Field Marshal Walther Brauchitsch, Commander-in-Chief of the German Army, that North Africa should be treated as a side show. Consequently, Rommel's pleas for additional men and material fell on deaf ears. Although the German High Command focused their eyes Eastward, it was upon Russia, not North Africa, that their gaze fell. Rommel, tirelessly, but in vain, attempted to convince them of the potential benefits possession of the Suez Canal could have for Germany. Halder, an old line traditionalist, tended to treat Rommel as a glory seeking upstart and was thus immune to his pleas and shunted his requests aside.

Churchill, on the other hand, took a direct interest in the planning and formulating of British military policy in North Africa and never hesitated to make suggestions on strategy, much to the dismay of his commanders in the field. His persistence, meddling, and constant pressure for taking the offensive had proven too much for Wavell and was subsequently to take its toll on Auchinleck as well.

It was precisely this type of interference which led to the newly developed battle plan, code-named "Crusader." Although the plan was on a much grander scale than the ill fated "Battleaxe," it was formulated in a manner strangly similiar to the latter and therefore not enthusiastically received by the British commanders in the field.

On November 18, Cunningham launched "Crusader" with an overwhelming superiority in men and material. During the formulation of the battle plan, Auchinleck suggested that Cunningham begin with a wide sweep around Rommel's desert flank. Strategically, it was a sound maneuver, but the British still failed to grasp the importance of massing their armour. As a result, the armour was broken up into scattered units.

Rommel meanwhile, had been contemplating an offensive of his own, aimed at the capture of Tobruk. The final preparations were being made when the first news of "Crusader" began filtering into his headquarters.

Rommel's first reaction was that the British attack was but a reconnaissance in force designed to upset his plans for Tobruk. But, within 24 hours, Sollum and Bradia were isolated and a dire threat to his flank was beginning to make itself known. Nevertheless, it was precisely this type of situation that had earned him his appropriate nickname, "The Desert Fox," for under pressure, facing a seemingly disastrous situation was just the time he was able to demonstrate his ability of turning certain defeat into a reverse for his opponent.

Leaving the Italian infantry formations with a few scattered German units to deal with the threat to his Northern flank, Rommel led the Afrika Korps into the desert to meet the rapidly developing threat in the South. Von Ravenstein of the 21 Panzer Division was already a prisoner of the British.

Major General Willoughby-Norrie of the XXX Corps was commanding the British formations threatening the Southern flank. Although he was advancing rapidly, he still failed to consolidate his armour, a fatal flaw when dealing with a man of Rommel's skill.

Rommel, at the head of his troops as usual, was quick to recognize Norrie's dispositions and began devising a counterstroke of his own. The Italian Ariete division was on a collision course with the British 22nd Armoured Brigade, and when the two collided head on, the Italians put up such a valiant fight that the British were compelled to withdraw.

Meanwhile, the Afrika Korps had begun a flanking movement of their own and managed to maneuver themselves south of the British formations. From there, they began exerting pressure on the British flanks, successfully turning the British spearheads northward. Norrie, finding himself in a pincer between the Afrika Korps in the South and the Italians in the North, contemplated withdrawal since by now, his formations were widely scattered over the desert with most of them having suffered heavily. Before he could receive confirmation from headquarters however, the unfortunate 5th South African Brigade was caught by the 15th Panzer Division near Sidi Rezegh and severely mauled.

Rommel, always the gambler, now sensed the momentum of battle was swinging in his favor and made the fatal decision that would ultimately cost him the battle. Leaving his operations officer, Siegfried Westphal to manage the battle in the North, he led the Afrika Korps off in a broad sweep into the British rear in the belief that could he but just reach the coast and sever the British line of supply and communications, he would be able to wreak havoc in their rear. Though a bold move, Rommel failed to reckon with the speed by which the British were able to regroup from their losses.

Cunningham, aware that Rommel was loose in his rear, panicked and requested Auchinleck to call off the offensive. In all fairness to Cunningham, it must be pointed out that he had never before faced an opponent as bold, wily, and unpredictable as Rommel. In addition, Cunningham's energy was sapped; he was a man totally worn out from the ordeal. Fortunately for the British, Auchinleck was not one easily alarmed and refused to accede to Cunningham's request. He did however, recognize Cunningham's inability to deal with the situation so, without further hesitation, he relieved the latter of command, sending forward his own Chief of Staff, General Sir Neil Ritchie, to take control of the situation.

The resupplied, reequipped, and newly led British responded by exerting pressure on the Axis forces holding the Northern end of the line. Westphal grudgingly began to yield ground in the face of superior opposition. Realizing that Rommel and the 21st Panzer Division were far away to the Southeast, far in the British rear, he called upon the 15th Panzer Division situated near Sidi-Rezegh where it was protecting Rommel's rear, to come to his aid. It was Westphal's willingness to assume command without confirming orders that saved the day for Panzerarmee Afrika. This performance typified the caliber of the German Desert Generals and was a tribute to Rommel's confidence in them. 15th Panzer Division, minus their commander, General Neumann-Silkow, killed in the fierce fighting near Sidi-Rezegh, complied with Westphal's request and charged to his assistance.

Meanwhile, Rommel, on his so called "dash to the wire," found himself deep in the British rear without support and running short of fuel and supplies. In addition, he had suffered heavy casualties that would be impossible to make good in his current position. His goal at the outset was the capture of British supplies with which his divisions would be able to live off of. Failing to accomplish this, he was forced to call off the thrust and order a retreat. Turning Westward, he made off toward his own lines. Though pursued by the British, he managed to reach his own positions without serious consequences.

During the retreat, one of the lighter episodes of the desert war took place which served to enhance the Rommel mystique among the British as the story was retold and magnified each time.

According to General Fritz Bayerlein who was riding with Rommel in his command vehicle, they were seemingly lost in the desert when they stumbled upon a New Zealand field hospital. Rommel wasted no time in jumping out of his car and strolling over to the hospital tent. Striking up a conversation with the head surgeon, he led the New Zealanders to believe that he had arrived at the head of an all conquering host of troops. He politely inquired as to the comfort of the wounded and assured the doctors that he would do all in his power to see to it that the wounded received every consideration in the way of water and medical supplies. Passing through the wards, he proceeded to shake hands with some of the wounded while praising their gallantry in action. Sauntering out the other side of the tent, he jumped into his staff car and was off before the befuddled New Zealanders realized that the commander of the entire Panzerarmee Afrika had been theirs for the taking.

Rommel realized that he would be unable to re-equip his forces in the field and, aware that with each passing day the British became stronger, decided to withdraw to his original positions at El Aghelia. He correctly reasoned that, protected by these fortifications, replenishment of those forces required to fight again, could proceed unimpaired. It was from this very position that he had originally begun his initial drive to the Egyptian border.

His withdrawal was in no way the disorganized rout so characteristic of the Italian retreat in 1940 or even the British retreat precipitated by Rommel's attack. The entire operation was carried out in an orderly and well organized fashion in the face of heavy enemy pressure. Pausing briefly at Gazala, Rommel lashed out at his tormentors long enough to convince Ritchie that he was still a force to be reckoned with. Though constantly harrassed by the British Air Forces, he demonstrated that he could be precise and methodical in conducting an orderly withdrawal even though his attacks could at times be considered reckless.

Ritchie's troops, although resupplied and re-equipped, had also fought themselves out and could offer little more than token resistance to Rommel's rear guards. By mid-December, Panzerarmee Afrika was back within its original positions with fortified lines to protect them. The British assessment was that the Axis troops had suffered heavily and would be unable to launch another offensive in the immediate future. Consequently, the 4th Indian Division and the green 1st Armoured Division were left to keep an eye on Rommel while the bulk of the British forces were withdrawn for refit.

Thanks to the British held Island of Malta and to Ultra, which told the British when and where the Axis convoys were sailing, much of the material desperately required by Rommel never reached him. However, despite the British effort, a meagre amount of supplies managed to trickle into the port of Tripoli. Although constituting no vast fortune in material, it proved sufficient to satisfy Rommel's immediate needs.

To the waiting and watching British forces, it seemed that the Desert Fox had hardly paused to catch his breath when on January 21, 1942, he came storming out of his positions and fell upon the forward British positions with fury.

Personally leading his troops as per usual, Rommel managed to drive a wedge between the unfortunate British divisions and advanced along the coast towards Agedabia. The following day, the 4th Indian Division was levered out of that position and by early the next morning the remainder of Rommel's forces managed to position themselves in front of the 1st Armoured Division near Saunna, encircling it on three sides. Although the Britishers fought heroically, they proved no match for the experienced, battle-hardened tank crews of the Afrika Korps. Fighting their way out of the trap, the 1st Armoured managed to extradite much of its man power but it ceased to exist as an effective fighting force.

Ritchie meanwhile, refused to take Rommel's threat seriously until reports of the severe mauling suffered by the unfortunate 1st Armoured began to arrive. From the time of his assumption of command, Ritchie operated under the handicap of being junior to his principle subordinate commanders in the field. His earlier failure to destroy Rommel had led many of these subordinates to have grave reservations about Ritchie as commander. His conduct of the battle now hardly inspired confidence in the officers of the newly designated 8th Army. As the situation rapidly deteriorated, confusing and contradictory orders began spewing forth from Ritchie's headquarters. Rommel's moves did nothing but apply more pressure on the already overburdened, confused, and dismayed Ritchie.

Moving out of Saunna towards Mechili in an apparent repetition of his earlier offensive, Rommel quickly reversed his field and drove rapidly on Benghazi. Ritchie's armour was positioned to thwart Rommel's thrust at Mechili, but this disposition served to isolate the 4th Indian Division at Benghazi. The hapless Indians now found themselves facing the entire might of the Afrika Korps. While Ritchie's armour was patiently waiting to strike a blow at the threat that in fact never materialized, the fate of the 4th Indian Division was sealed. Although they did manage to break through the thin cordon encircling them, in their haste the Indians failed to destroy large dumps of supplies that were captured virtually intact along with the key port of Benghazi.

When report of casualties reached Ritchie's 8th Army Headquarters, he at first simply refused to believe them. Once confirmation of these reports verified the loss, Ritchie lost control of the entire front. He began issuing confusing and contradictory orders which not only failed to alleviate the situation, but instead, accelerated the loss of confidence felt by Ritchie's subordinates on his ability to intelligently conduct the flow of the battle. Perplexity now became the order of the day at 8th Army Headquarters. It seemed as if Ritchie had succumbed to the myth that the "Desert Fox" was some sort of Bogey Man that was mysteriously invincible. Fortunately again for the British, Auchinleck, refusing to allow emotions to dictate the flow of the battle, arrived at 8th Army Headquarters in time to avert total disaster. Despite the urgings of the British Corps commanders, Auchinleck refused to sack Ritchie. The British Commander-in-Chief was of the opinion that merely changing commanders just as one changes a pair of socks was not the answer to defeating Rommel. Mindful of the painful decision it had been relieving Cunningham during "Crusader," he desired no repetition of that distasteful experience. Instead, the talented General Godwin-Austin of XII Corps was relieved after offering Auchinleck a "Ritchie or Me" ultimatum.

Rommel's decision to pause after the fall of Benghazi was dictated by the fact that he was suffering an acute supply shortage. Although somewhat alleviated by the capture of stores at Benghazi, another sustained offensive was clearly out of the question for the time being. However, as a reward for the short but spec-

131

tacular campaign, Hitler promoted Rommel to the rank of Colonel General.

Rommel's superb conduct of the North African campaign to this point did not fail to leave an indelible mark on Sir Winston Churchill. The great leader who so vehemently despised anything even remotely associated with Hitler and Nazism paid the supreme tribute to Rommel while addressing Parliament in late January when he said, "We have a very daring and skillful opponent against us, and may I say across the havoc of war, a great general."[2]

On February 15, Rommel left the desert for Germany to report his future intentions to Hitler. After a brief overnight visit to his family, he flew on to Hitler's headquarters where he was warmly received by the Fuhrer of the German Reich.

Command of the Desert forces was left in the very capable hands of General Ludwig Cruewell who was succeeded as commander of the Afrika Korps by a newcomer to the desert, General Walther Nehring, a veteran Panzer commander who now began a career that would see him become one of the finest Corps commanders of either side during World War II.

It was Rommel's intention while at Hitler's Headquarters to request of the High Command additional reinforcements for the forthcoming campaign. He further wished to discuss with them the possibility of neutralizing Malta. Unfortunately for Rommel, the effects of the Russian venture and the attitude of the Generals at

OKW* who still considered him an impertinent upstart, played a decisive role in the denial of his requests. Despite the lukewarm reception given to him by his military comrades, Hitler's enthusiastic welcome proved encouraging. The latter promised Rommel that he would do everything in his power to assist. With that assurance, the jealous generals at OKW agreed to assist Rommel and Field Marshal Albert Kesselring, Commander-in-Chief South, was assigned to formulate a plan for the capture of Malta. Recognizing the threat posed by British naval and air forces based on that island, they went so far as to promise airborne troops for an assault on this dangerous thorn in the Axis side.

Upon returning to the desert, Rommel immediately began drafting plans for renewing the offensive. Although already in a short space of time he had achieved a spectacular reputation, his next campaign was to be hailed as a masterpiece of mobile warfare; firmly cementing his reputation as a brilliant and daring commander.

The obstacles facing Panzerarmee Afrika were quite formidable. The British had constructed a lengthy defensive position from Gazala on the coast, 40 miles southward into the desert terminating at a defensive position known as Bir Hakim. The layout of the Gazala line was based on a series of infantry brigade defensive boxes sited in suitable areas of desert which had some

*Oberkommando der Wermacht Supreme Command of the Armed Forces

tactical significance. Each box was given a defensive perimeter of mines and wire, behind which the defending troops were dug in, being covered by anti-tank guns and field artillery. In the North, these boxes were well mined and within mutual supporting distance of each other. As one proceeded South, the line became more tenuous with a gap of 5 miles between the northern defenses and the box of the 150th Brigade of the 50th Division. South of the 150th Brigade, there was little but minefields for the 10 mile stretch to Bir Hakim at the southern terminus of the Gazala line.

Ritchie had concluded that Rommel would either attack along the coastal route or attempt to cut his way through the minefields behind which the British armoured formations were poised, ready to strike a decisive blow should Rommel succeed.

One fatal flaw dominated Ritchie's plan and Rommel quickly spotted where it was. The Bir Hakim box was not only immobile, but isolated at the southern end of the line and unsupported by any other force. A wide flanking movement around the position could, if successful, present the unprecedented opportunity for rolling up the entire British rear. Characteristically, Rommel selected this route for his advance.

To accomplish his task, Rommel reasoned quite correctly that all supporting units would be required to coordinate their assignments with a minimum of error. His supplies too, would have to keep pace with the advance. Thanks to the aerial assault against Malta over the previous few months, his supply situation was vastly improved although he was not wealthy in this area. It would be totally necessary for these vital stores to maintain pace with the advancing assault units. Four days was Rommel's estimate for completion of the battle, provided the rigid timetable was strictly adhered to.

Rommel, the fox, now tried to deceive Ritchie as to his avenue of advance. Using large fans mounted on camouflaged vehicles which the Germans drove round the front and center of the British positions attempting to stir up clouds of dust, they left the impression that large formations of armour were on the move in these areas. It was hoped that this tactic would completely deceive Ritchie and firm up his convictions as to the route of Rommel's advance. Also in the North, Cruewell, commanding the Italian infantry formations with some German support units, was directed to launch an attack during the unlikely time of mid-afternoon on the chosen day, May 26. Initially it was to be merely a diversionary tactic which could be later followed up by a major assault once Rommel was loose in the British rear.

How could Ritchie be fooled since Ultra should have made him aware that Rommel was practicing deception? The answer to this question is simple. Ritchie was not aware of Ultra. This might sound utterly ridiculous but the British had some firm reasons for not letting Ritchie in on the secret. Because of the fluidity of desert fighting and the eavesdropping of each other's wireless channels, it was decided that no front line general would be allowed to see, possess, or even know of Ultra. The danger of capture was too great, already in the two years of desert fighting, numbers of British front line generals including General O'Connor had been captured. In Cairo, only three people knew of Ultra; Auchinleck, his Director of Military Operations, and General Francis de Guigand, the Director of Military Intelligence.

General Sir Neil Ritchie was not allowed to view Ultras. If the contents of an Ultra were deemed of sufficient importance to his battle planning, either Auchinleck acquainted him with the information via letter while never revealing the source or, De Guigand would fly to the commander's headquarters to brief Ritchie personally. Of course there was always the danger that Ritchie might reject the information in the assumption that his own local intelligence was better and more current.

Ultra had given Auchinleck ample knowledge of Rommel's intention to attack and of his objectives. When Auchinleck forwarded his appreciation to Ritchie, the latter, unaware of Auchinleck's source of information, ignored it in the belief that his own local intelligence was superior. Thus Ritchie fought Rommel without benefit of his greatest weapon, Ultra. The British were condemned to fight piecemeal in scattered armoured formations.

Rommel's attack began on May 26, 1942 in the

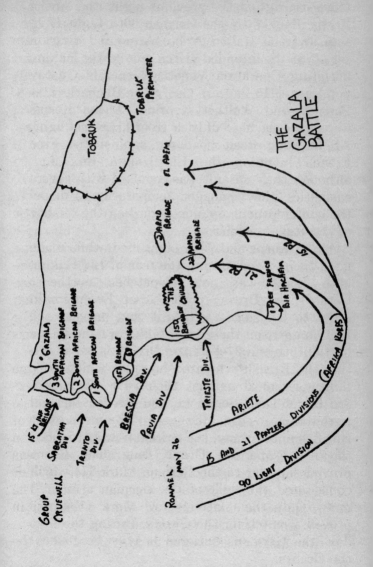

THE GAZALA BATTLE

North during daylight hours exactly as planned. However, during the previous night, the Afrika Korps, flanked by the German 90th Light Division and the Italian Ariete Armoured division set off on the intended march around Bir Hakim, initiating Operation Venetia. Generals Gustav von Vaerst (15 Panzer), Georg von Bismark (21st Panzer), and Walther Nehring (Afrika Korps) were all at the head of their troops. At first light, Ariete flung itself headlong against the Free French manning the Bir Hakim Box and, although their assault was repulsed with severe casualties, they managed temporarily to dispel the contemptuous opinion regarding the quality of the Italian soldier.

Afrika Korps and 90th Light meanwhile made good their swing around the rear of Bir Hakim. 90th Light was now dispatched northeast towards the British positions at El Adem in order to lay siege to Tobruk and prevent the British garrison there from taking a hand in the battle. 15th and 21st Panzer Divisions began hitting the British armoured brigades which were flung piecemeal against them. 4th Armoured, 3rd Royal Tank Regiment, and 8th Hussars; all were routed in turn. However to Rommel's great surprise and dismay, the British now introduced the new American Grant Tank. The Grant proved superior to the German Mark III which constituted the bulk of the German armoured units. Only the relatively few Mark IV tanks proved a match for the Grants. During the first day, the Germans suffered heavily because of the Grants.

Norrie, commanding the British armour, wisely pulled back and out of line in order to avoid having his forces destroyed. The result was that Rommel, in his drive to the coast parallel with the British rear, would now find the by-passed British armour situated on his flank.

In addition to the heavy losses suffered by the Afrika Korps during the first two days of fighting, the box at Bir Hakim remained intact and forays from that position managed to harass the German supply columns. Those supply convoys that successfully eluded the Bir Hakim position in their attempt to keep pace with the Afrika Korps were set upon by the British armoured formations.

Rommel's situation became perilous. The British armour commanded his right flank, the static positions (minefields interspersed with boxes) held his left flank, and a strong position at Bir Hakim dominated his rear. Furthermore, Cruewell's frontal assault in the North had gone awry when the commander himself was captured after his reconnaisance plane was shot down behind enemy lines. The loss of Cruewell was a particularly bitter pill for Rommel to swallow. Even though Field Marshal Albert Kesselring arrived at Cruewell's headquarters and offered to assume command and subordinate himself to Rommel, the situation was beyond salvation.

Rommel now gambled. On the surface to the military student his action appears to be at the very least, a calculated risk, Rommel possessed an almost uncanny instinct to read his opponents' mind and had mastered the ability to use this instinct to outguess the opposing commander. He correctly deduced that Ritchie would exercise caution in attempting to destroy the Afrika Korps and he thus used this as a basis for his next decision.

The 90th Light Division, under General Kleeman, was ordered to fight their way back from El Adem and link up with the Afrika Korps. Ariete, 15th and 21st Panzer divisions were directed to consolidate a position with their backs to the British minefields and dig in facing their antagonists. Nehring, digging in his 88's, laid down a devastating flak barrage in the face of probing British armour, successfully protecting the withdrawal of Rommel.

May 30 found Rommel in his chosen positions with 90th Light rejoined to him. This area of the desert was now to become famous as the "Cauldron" which would prove as tough for the British as Tobruk had proven for Rommel. It was Rommel's intention to lay in the Cauldron while a path could be cut in the minefields through which supplies and reinforcements would be able to reach the beleaguered Afrika Korps. The Italian Trieste Division promptly complied and cut the necessary corridor.

Unfortunately, directly astride this path in the center of the line, sat the box manned by the British 150th Brigade. Situated as it was, it could effectively prevent supplies from moving up. It was soon evident that the British position would have to be eliminated if the Afrika Korps was to salvage the situation. Supply problems, especially water, was becoming rapidly critical and capitulation a distinct possibility.

Rommel however, refused to relinquish the initiative and sent Bismark's 21st Panzer Division in a devastating assault on the box. Wave after wave of attack was beaten off. It took Rommel's personal leadership to defeat and overcome the British resistance. During the fighting, Rommel led one of the assaults personally. The British were not selling their lives cheaply. Finally, Rommel ordered his men to wave their white flag in the hope that the 150th Brigade in their box at Got el Ualab would capitulate, which they promptly did and marched into captivity. The Afrika Korps supply situation was now somewhat alleviated, but there still remained the question of Bir Hakim.

A decision was made that the French position must be neutralized just as the 150th Brigade box was. Rommel sent the relatively fresh Trieste Division to accomplish this task. Stukas provided by Kesselring who was anxious to end the fighting so that Malta could be dealt with once and for all, began to soften up the French position in anticipation of Rommel's forthcoming attack. Although the Stukas exacted a fearful toll, they in turn incurred heavy casualties at the hands of the more maneuverable British planes.

Meanwhile, Ritchie launched a series of uncoordinated attacks against the "Cauldron" in the area believed manned by Ariete. But the

British had once again miscalculated and instead ran headlong into the 15th and 21st Panzer Divisions. The Afrika Korps, under the redoubtable Nehring, successfully beat off these attacks with a minimum of difficulty, nullifying the British threat. Once again, Nehring had used his panzers to lure the British tanks onto the sights of his dug in 88's where the withering fire took a heavy toll of life and British tanks.

When Trieste finally launched their attack on Bir Hakim, the French troops, though sorely punished by German aerial assault, were still a defiant group of warriors. Incredibly, although Bir Hakim was completely isolated and beseiged, Ritchie made no attempt to come to its assistance. After beating off a number of assaults, amassing heavy casualties and nearly out of supplies, the gallant Frenchmen requested permission to break out of the trap. On the night of June 10, General Pierre Koenig, the brave and daring French commander, marched his valiant troops out of the Bir Hakim box and set off for Egypt, leaving only a small rearguard and his wounded behind in the firm belief that the latter would suffer no hardship at the hands of the "Desert Fox." On the morning of June 11, Bir Hakim was taken by probing elements of Trieste.

Almost simultaneously with the fall of Bir Hakim, the now revitalized Afrika Korps came roaring out of the Cauldron like all the banshees of hell. The British outposts were swiftly overrun and each British unit guarding the Gazala

Line was taken on in turn by the advancing Afrika Korps. The once imposing Gazala Line, containing over forty miles of fortifications, now became untenable. Disorganized units of the 8th Army began streaming back towards Tobruk and the Egyptian border in a wild, confused rout. The British 7th Armoured Division, "The Desert Rats," ceased to exist as an effective fighting unit and 22nd Armoured Brigade was virtually destroyed. Even more crucial, the Afrika Korps was rapidly approaching the coast in an effort to cut off both 50th Division and 1st South African Division. In the Knightsbridge box, the Guards Brigade was quickly overrun during the German dash towards the coast. The 1st South African Division fought their way out along the Via Balba, avoiding a complete encirclement, but it was forced to leave all its heavy weapons behind. 50th Division, finding their avenue of retreat barred, attacked westward against the Italians. Although they succeeded in breaking through, they were compelled to traverse the entire length of the Gazala line southward into the desert, a maneuver that was brilliantly executed, but which effectively took this division completely out of the fighting during their retreat to Egypt.

Finding themselves on the coast with the Gazala positions abandoned by the British, the original German plan called for an assault against Malta. However, Rommel, realizing that a smashing victory had been won, insisted on exploiting the situation.

Kesselring, Mussolini and the Italian Commando Supremo opted for adherence to the original plan and pressured Rommel to do likewise. However, because of his amazing string of victories, Rommel had the respect and the ear of Hitler who was mesmerized by the former's apparent mastery of the North African campaign. It was therefore an easy task for Rommel to convince Hitler that to pause now would constitute folly. The German Dictator, never one for heeding the advice of his military strategists, decided in favor of Rommel and used his influence to exert pressure on the Italians, insisting that they accede to his favorite general's demands. Furthermore, Hitler was fearful of using airborne troops at Malta. The heavy casualties incurred by these troops in the attack against Crete still haunted the Fuhrer. The Italians, supported by Kesselring, reluctantly gave way; but not before the Commander-in-Chief South emphatically warned of the dire consequences this decision could produce.

Thus Malta was to be ignored temporarily and the German Air Fleet in Italy was directed to support Rommel's drive to the Nile.

Driving his weary troops unmercifully, Rommel set off in pursuit of the routed 8th Army. His rapid advance continued on past Tobruk, leaving with Auchinleck the impression that the Germans once more intended to merely lay siege to that port such as had been done earlier. Auchinleck, against his better judgment and in violation of his previous plans, rushed what precious few reinforcements that could be scraped together into Tobruk at the express demand of Churchill who, in a very forceful tone, stated that under no circumstances must Tobruk fall to the Axis.

But Rommel's lightning advance did not allow the defenders time to repair the formerly strong defensive system, the same one which had held the Germans at bay for so long the previous year. The defensive perimeter around the city had been neglected during the preceding months in order to reinforce the Gazala line. In many places, even the anti-tank ditches were filled in to facilitate supply convoys moving up from Egypt.

Leaving the Italian infantry formations to demonstrate against the Western section of the Tobruk perimeter, Rommel broke through the sadly manned Eastern defenses. Taking control of the Afrika Korps himself, Rommel personally led the assault. At one point, while driving along the desert seeking a position for his headquarters, Rommel sighted several empty German trucks. Realizing that he had come upon a belt of mines, he nonchalantly lifted himself from the car and personally knelt down and began carefully lifting the mines with his own hands. His personal staff quickly followed suit and within five minutes, the mine belt was cleared away.

The final assault began on the morning of June 20. Although the defenders put up an admirable resistance, Rommel's sheer weight of armour proved too much for the British to handle. The next morning, Tobruk, the symbol of determined resistance, fell like a ripe piece of fruit to the Afrika Korps. One day was all Rommel had required. So swift was his coup, that the defenders were unable to destroy the vast amount of stores contained in the port. These now became welcome booty for the Afrika Korps. It was a great day for Rommel. Hitler's elation at this latest victory held no bounds and he promoted Rommel to Field Marshal on the spot. The Desert Fox, at age 51, became the youngest Field Marshal in the German Army.

By now Rommel had become for the British, somewhat of a Bogey Man. Auchinleck sensed the magical effect Rommel's name was having among his forces and knew that he must dispel this bewitchment it held among his men. Therefore he issued the following message:

"There exists a real danger that our friend Rommel is becoming a kind of magician or bogey-man to our troops, who are talking far too much about him. He is by no means a superman, although he is undoubtedly very energetic and able. Even if he were a superman, it would still be highly undesirable that our men should credit him with supernatural powers.

I wish you to dispel by all possible means the idea that Rommel represents something more than an ordinary German general. The important thing now is to see that we do not always talk of Rommel when we mean the enemy in Libya. We must refer to "the Germans" of "the Axis Powers," or "the enemy" and not always keep harping on Rommel.

Please be sure that this order is put into immediate effect, and impress upon all commanders that from a psychological point of view, it is a matter of highest importance."[3]

Now Rommel was plunging headlong toward the Egyptian border. Ritchie meanwhile, managed to rally the disorganized British columns near Mersa Matruh but once more placed his units in static positions, although he did finally concentrate his armour. But, they were positioned south of Mersa Matruh and were exhausted and depleted after having suffered badly during the previous fighting.

90th Light Division, which played no role in the assault on Tobruk but instead had continued on along the coast road, managed to slip behind the British units at Mersa Matruh, once again cutting the avenue of escape. Meanwhile Rommel began to reach out for the Nile. However, in the heady atmosphere of victory, with the Nile staring him in the face, he failed to take into account the limits of human endurance. This had the effect of slowing and eventually halting the Axis at a new defensive line established by the British forces at El Alamein.

The purpose of this chapter has been to enlighten the reader regarding Rommel's great victory at Gazala and Tobruk which has hopeful-

MEDITERRANEAN SEA

TO TRIPOLI

EL AGHEILA

BEDA FOMM

BENGHAZI

MECHILI

DERNA

GAZALA

TOBRUK

EL ADEM

BARDIA

CAPUZZO

BUQ BUQ

SIDI BARRANI

MERSA MATRUH

MARTUH

EL ALAMEIN

ALEXANDRIA

HALFAYA

TO CAIRO

ly been accomplished. However, in order to broaden the perspective and make this chapter complete, we have intentionally included material about Rommel prior to Gazala. Now we shall attempt to expose the reader to Rommel after Gazala. In order to do so, the limit we now place on the rest of this chapter must be understood. If we were to attempt to write in depth about Rommel after Gazala, this chapter itself could conceiveably constitute an entire book.

The Gazala battles, terminating with the fall of Tobruk had unquestionably been Rommel's greatest achievement, firmly cementing his position among the great captains of history. His opening moves were a masterpiece of deception and would have exercised an even greater influence on the battle had it not been for Cruewell's untimely capture. The race around Bir Hakim had taken the British completely by surprise. His decision to withdraw into the Cauldron was the supreme stroke. In the face of firm opposition, he sat with his back to the British position, supremely confident that the enemy would be unable to lever him out of his chosen position. His ability to correctly gauge the mind of his opponent allowed him to first defeat the 150th Brigade and then the Bir Hakim position without opposition from Ritchie. Finally, no one, particularly Ritchie, dared dream that Rommel could lay in the Cauldron, in the face of superior force, and regain the initiative. To most military experts, another offensive by

Rommel was totally out of the question.

Rommel's conduct of the operation gave the impression to the world that he was faced with a group of bumbling incompetents. Quite the contrary was in reality the truth. The British Corps commanders had all demonstrated flashes of brilliance at times, but their command structure did not allow for maneuver on their own recognizance which hampered their control of the battle by demanding headquarters approval for and deviation from the fixed plan of battle and restricted their many opportunities presented by the fluid state of the battlefield.

Rommel, on the other hand, maintained a relatively loose rein over his subordinate commanders, allowing them the necessary flexibility to use their own initiative as each opportunity occurred. Furthermore, it was the habit of the British to conduct the battle from static headquarters far behind the lines while Rommel and his commanders were masters at leading from the front as evidenced by the many casualties suffered by general officers during the North African campaign.

Finally, the procession of Eighth Army commanders simply proved no match for the wily and clever Rommel. Cunningham showed brief flashes of brilliance in Eritrea but was worn out by the time he was brought in to oppose Rommel. Ritchie was the wrong man from the very start. With virtually no prior experience, he was thrown into the fray over the heads of senior and more talented subordinates. His lack of knowledge regarding mobile warfare and use of armour were to have a dramatic effect on the conduct of the battles. It was a gross injustice to expect this man to be able to compete on even terms with the Desert Fox. In fairness to the man, however, he subsequently went forth to lead a Corps in Europe with distinction, being personally selected by General Montgomery.

Now let us pick up the threads of combat with the forces moving towards El Alamein.

With the British retreating to Alamein after having escaped near certain destruction at Mersa Matruh, the Afrika Korps mercilessly pursued them deep into Egypt. On towards El Alamein drove Rommel. Auchinleck finally grasped the reins of the Eighth Army with his own hands. Alamein geographically formed an excellent position since it prohibited a flanking movement a la Gazala. At one end of the line was the Mediterranean Sea and at the other sat the impassable Quattara Depression.

Auchinleck wasted little time in preparing the line and hurridly rushed reinforcements forward from Cairo. He realized that should this line fall, Egypt's fate would be sealed and with it that of the Suez Canal, the great Naval base at Alexandria, and the Mideast oil supplies.

It was a weary and much understrength Panzerarmee Afrika that brushed up against the Alamein positions on June 30. The British line failed to break and Rommel was finally, but reluctantly, forced to call a halt.

But the Desert Fox proved as stubborn as he

was cunning and a brief pause was all he allowed. With the pitifully few reinforcements available to him, Rommel once more assailed the British line. Fatigue now began to take the measure of the Desert Fox and his previous brilliance seemed to desert him. Forced by sheer exhaustion to rely on the use of past tactics, his moves were obvious to Auchinleck. Besides, Ultra exposed Rommel completely to the British who by now were using this intelligence more wisely.

In one final effort on July 3, the Afrika Korps battered themselves against the Alamein line. After some initial headway, it became apparent that their strength had eroded enough to prohibit a successful assault. The movements of Rommel were known through Ultra by Auchinleck, and as each opportunity presented itself, strong counter-attacks were directed against the Afrika Korps, effectively checkmating them. Auchinleck devised the strategy of attacking the Italian formations while Rommel was on the move, forcing the latter to call off his attack and rush to the aid of his beleaguered allies. In retrospect, Auchinleck's conduct during the first Battle of Alamein was exemplary.

Obviously the British had profited from their devastating experience at Gazala and were preparing for another encounter at Alamein. One of the British "casualties" in the preparations for the next confrontation was Auchinleck himself. He was replaced by a man destined to become one of the Allies' greatest generals, Sir Harold Alexander. To command 8th Army, Montgomery arrived and began to "set things right," his favorite expression. Although Montgomery had been second choice (General Gott, the first choice was killed in a plane crash while on his way to assume command of 8th Army), the appointment proved fortunate for the British.

Montgomery refused to be badgered into a premature offensive by Churchill and incredibly got away with it. When he did finally launch the offensive, it was with such superiority of man and material that victory was a foregone conclusion. Also, the British finally grasped the significance of Ultra, informing Montgomery about its existence almost immediately.

By the summer of 1942, the fortunes of the Germans were changing. Rommel's intelligence sources, the Black Code, the Condor Mission, (a spy network in Cairo) were all discovered and now turned against him. The supply situation also favored the British.

From England, convoys sailed in relative safety around the southern tip of Africa and disembarked their precious cargoes at Red Sea ports. From there, it was a simple matter to move the supplies overland to Egypt. On the other hand, the Axis forces were forced to rely on convoys from Italy to supply their needs. The Royal Navy and the Royal Air Force squadrons stationed at Malta so completely held sway over control of the Mediterranean that it was the exception rather than the rule when a convoy from Italy reached Tripoli safely. Again Ultra came to the Allies' aid, giving them the route and type of supplies being sent. Usually, less than half of the supplies destined for North Africa reached their goal. Those that finally did reach Tripoli, were required to traverse miles of scorching desert enroute to the front. On this trip, supply convoys were subjected to constant attack by the Royal Air Force from Malta. More than any amount of ships or planes, Malta's influence on operations in that theatre of war contributed to Rommel's ultimate defeat. Kesselring's dire prediction had indeed proven true.

When Montgomery finally launched his long anticipated offensive, Rommel was away in Germany for a much deserved rest and cure of the sores and glandular problems that had seriously threatened his health during the latter stages of the Alamein campaign. Ironically, General Georg Stumme whom Rommel had superseded as commander of the 7th Panzer Division in France was appointed to deputize during the latter's absence. Rommel wisely requested General Heinz Guderian as his replacement but unfortunately, the great Panzer leader was out of favor at the time. In addition, Nehring had been wounded before Alamein and General Ritter von Thoma, an experienced panzer general was dispatched to North Africa as his replacement.

On October 23, 1943, British artillery began firing all along the front, marking the beginning of Montgomery's offensive. The battle must be examined from the point of view of Montgomery's handiwork.

Superiority in numbers would of course play a great part in the British victory. But superiority in deception and battlefield intelligence contributed equally. Knowing full well that he possessed a marked superiority, Montgomery retired to bed prior to the attack, leaving the conduct of the battle to his subordinates. The unfortunate Stumme found himself unable to stem the rapidly rising tide, although he did manage to upset Montgomery's timetable somewhat. However, the result of the battle was a foregone conclusion.

Rommel, hearing of the attack, quickly set off to resume his command. Upon his return he found the situation in turmoil. Stumme was dead from heart failure at the front and von Thoma was now conducting the battle. Immediately grasping the seriousness of the situation, Rommel wired Hitler for permission to withdraw in the face of overwhelming odds. But the Fuhrer refused permission for even a slight step backward. Victory or death was the motto adopted by the demented German leader. Although thoroughly disillusioned by Hitler's telegram, Rommel's first instinct was to heed his soldierly code and obey orders without objection. But, in the face of Montgomery's overwhelming strength, he refused to sacrifice those troops that had served him so well; so he sanctioned a withdrawal on his own recognizance. Hitler subsequently upheld this decision.

Meanwhile the Allied landings in Northwest Africa on November 8 represented a dire threat to Rommel's main supply port at Tripoli. It left him with no choice but to execute a long retreat in order to protect his only means of support. Montgomery followed at a safe distance, always conscious that Rommel had frequently before turned certain defeat into sudden victory by turning on his tormentors and exacting swift retribution from those British generals who proved too bold. Each time Rommel was forced to pause from lack of fuel or to rest, Montgomery settled down to insure his superiority remained intact. This respite allowed the Desert Fox to successfully slip away and withdraw to the Mareth Line in Tunisia with a minimum of interference. Once behind the Mareth Line, Rommel, secure in the knowledge that Montgomery would once again settle down to await his supplies, turned on the green American troops at Kasserine Pass.

On February 19, 1943, Rommel inflicted severe losses on the first United States troops in the European theatre. Fortunately for the Americans, General Hans Jurgen von Arnim, commanding the German forces in Tunisia, refused to cooperate with Rommel and the Germans were unable to exploit their success. Incredibly, although reinforcements were unavailable for Rommel at Alamein, von Arnim received more in the way of reinforcements and supplies than Rommel had received for his entire campaign in the desert.

With certain defeat staring him in the face from the Americans in Tunisia and with the British ready to assault the Mareth Line, on March 9, Rommel left Africa for good, leaving von Arnim in total command. It was only a relatively short time before this arrogant commander was compelled to surrender his forces to the Allies on May 13.

After turning command in Tunisia over to Von Arnim, Rommel arrived in Germany and immediately resumed the treatments for his deteriorating health which were cut short by the crisis at El Alamein. While undergoing these treatments, Rommel watched with mounting sadness the plight of his former comrades in arms in North Africa. During this period, he began to have reservations about Hitler's ability to conduct the war, even to the point of suspecting that the latter was no longer capable of making intelligent decisions.

With his convalescence ended, he was temporarily assigned to Hitler's staff until a suitable command became available. In this capacity, he was able to speak frequently with the Feuher. These conversations only served to convince Rommel that Hitler himself suspected the war was now a lost cause.

July 1943 found Rommel off to Greece to command the Balkan area when it was suspected that the Allies were contemplating an invasion there. With hardly enough time to unpack, Rommel was redirected to the Alps after Mussolini's overthrow. It was Hitler's conviction that a number of divisions stationed in the Alps north of Italy could react swiftly and disarm the Italians should they decide to surrender to the Allies.

With the invasion of Italy imminent, it was decided to appoint one commander for all of Italy. After deciding on Rommel, Hitler abruptly changed his mind at the last moment and appointed Kesselring to this post. History was to judge that his instincts were once again to be rewarded.

With Kesselring now in overall command of Italy, Rommel was reassigned to Inspector General of the Atlantic Wall in November of 1943. Although no troops were his to command, Rommel immediately set about the task of making the Atlantic Wall impregnable.

Instinct told him that the Allies would attempt their invasion in a number of places, Normandy being one of the possible areas, so he wasted little time in designing and preparing defenses to meet the approaching assault. Underwater obstacles, countless numbers of mines, stakes planted in the ground to foil glider and parachute operations and mile upon mile of barbed wire were feverishly assembled. At the beginning of 1944, Rommel once more resumed active command. Army Group B was assigned to him, coincidently in the area where he was currently installing some of his strongest obstacles, Normandy. Although subordinate to the Commander-in-Chief West, Gerd von Rundstedt, as a Field Marshal, Rommel was entitled to direct access to Hitler. Fortunately for the Allies, Hitler disagreed with Rommel's choice of the potential invasion site. Hitler was expertly being duped by the Allied deception plans under the overall name of Operation Bodyguard. Bodyguard's basic goal was to deceive Hitler into thinking that the invasion would take place in a number of different places, the prime one being the Pas de Calais.

In addition, Rundstedt and Rommel differed over tactical dispositions. Rommel, having experienced first hand what devastating effect allied air supremacy could have on a battle, insisted that the mobile panzer reserves be stationed near the front so that an Allied landing could be met head on and defeated before it was possible to establish a bridgehead. Von Rundstedt however, insisted on allowing the Allies to come ashore and drive inland where their spearheads could easily be defeated by the panzers being held away from the coast.

On June 6, 1944, the Allied invasion of Normandy began while Rommel was away in Germany. Returning to the front immediately, Rommel urgently requested support from the panzer reserve force positioned many miles inland. Hitler, supported by von Rundstedt, refused on the basis that the Normandy attack was merely a feint and that the real invasion, to be commanded by General Patton, was yet to come. Rommel was condemmed to fight an uneven battle.

By the time von Rundstedt was able to come

to grips with the situation, the Allied bridgehead was firmly established and secure. Although later in the the month both Field Marshals attempted to gain Hitler's authorization for a partial withdrawal. Hitler refused with his customary no withdrawal obstinence. Von Rundstedt and Rommel were now appearing to Hitler as defeatists.

On July 17, 1944, Rommel was riding in his staff car near Army Group B Headquarters at LaRoche Guyon, when the car was set upon by a group of strafing Canadian planes. His driver was seriously wounded causing the vehicle to overturn, throwing Rommel out into the road. Two of his traveling companions managed to transport the critically wounded Field Marshal to a local French physician where his lacerations were attended to and then on to a German Field Hospital a few miles away. Upon examination it was determined by the physicians that Rommel had suffered a serious skull fracture, placing his very life in serious jeopardy. Although unconscious for a few days, his magnificent will power refused to give in and soon the indomitable leader was up and about. However, the convalescence would be a lengthy one.

During his recuperation period, word came to Rommel that an attempt to assassinate Hitler had been undertaken but had been successfully thwarted with only minor injuries to the Fuhrer. He later learned of the brutal recriminations taken by Hitler on those in any way implicated in the plot.

Rommel had been aware of the plot since February of that year although he was not informed that the conspirators would attempt to kill Hitler. During conversations with his old friend, Dr. Karl Strolin, the Mayor of Stuttgart, the subject had been broached and Rommel ventured the opinion that Hitler's death would only serve to make a martyr of the man and that arrest and trial was the only obvious answer. Nevertheless, the conspirators, including Dr. Strolin, went about their plans for ridding Germany of Hitler. As a possible successor to the German leader, a man with equal stature and popularity would have to be selected. Only one man in all of Germany fit that description; Rommel. Even Rommel's Chief of Staff, General Hans Speidel had taken an active role in the conspiracy since its inception. He attempted to influence Rommel into assuming a more active role but the latter was reluctant to participate in any plot that included Hitler's murder. He did however, agree that Hitler had to go.

Though recuperating from his wounds, Rommel's name was mentioned as having been involved in the plot. On October 14, under the pretense of wishing to discuss a future command, Generals Ernst Maisel and Wilhelm Burgdorf arrived from Berlin at Rommel's home. During the course of their secluded discussion, Rommel was offered the opportunity to take his own life. The alternative was a trial before a court in Berlin. If Rommel were to select the latter alternative, the future safety of his family, should he be found guilty, could not be guaranteed by the two generals. Should however, he select the former alternative and take his own life, he could be assured of not only his family's safety, but also a state funeral complete with full military honors and all the trappings. Quite naturally, Rommel opted for the former alternative.

After saying his farewells to his family and staff, Rommel drove off with Maisel and Burgdorf. A short time later word was received by the local army commandant that Field Marshall Erwin Rommel, at the age of 53, had suffered an attack and was dead. The official announcement stated that the Field Marshal had succumbed to his wounds.

At the pompous state ceremony held in Rommel's honor, Field Marshal Gerd von Rundstedt read the officially prepared eulogy and a day of mourning was declared throughout Germany.

Thirty years later, Hitler's name still lives in infamy and Nazism is synonymous with massive brutal murder. But the name the "Desert Fox" and Rommel are legendary and still revered, not only in Germany, but the Western world as well. No other person in recent history has managed to capture the imagination and command the respect that surrounds the name, "The Desert Fox." Indeed, he may accurately be described as the last bastion of the age of chivalry on the battlefield.

The post-war years have given birth to a relative handful of critics of Rommel's ability.

Some have been so audacious as to claim that Rommel's ability did not exceed the level of Corps commander. Utter nonsense! The present chapter has hopefully dispelled that erroneous and unjust estimation.

Field Marshal Erich von Manstein

Chapter 4

November of 1942 is remembered by the Germans as a dark period for the German Army. Its crack Sixth Army was surrounded by the Soviets at Stalingrad and there existed a possibility that an entire Army Group would fall like a ripe piece of fruit into the anticipating hands of a victory starved Soviet Army. Given this potential, Hitler turned to one of his most formidable Field Marshals to salvage the crumbling situation. If anyone were to save the day, it would be this military genius. Even von Paulus and the Sixth Army allowed themselves to feel optimistic, perhaps the situation was not beyond salvation. For Field Marshal Fritz Erich von Manstein had just been appointed to command the newly created Army Group Don, whose task it was to bring the enemy attack to a standstill and recapture the positions previously occupied by the German Army.

Fritz Erich von Manstein was a typical product of the great German General Staff. His obvious talent, observed during the Great War, secured him a position in the post World War I German Army. Like many of his colleagues, the between war period was spent in a variety of staff roles. By 1938, von Manstein had risen t/ the post of Deputy Chief of the General Sta'f. However, because of the Fritsch affair wh'ch caused the retirement of many senior officers,* Manstein was sent off to command an infantry division.

When it became apparent that Hitler's sword rattling would most certainly precipitate war, many of the retired senior generals were recalled to active duty, among them Gerd von Rundstedt, who was posted to command an army group during the Czech crisis and the subsequent invasion of the Sudentenland. Von Manstein was appointed von Rundstedt's Chief of Staff.

The harmonious working relationship developed between the two generals during this period led to the formation of a formidable command setup which greatly enhanced the performance of the army group during the Polish campaign, where it played a leading role. It was during this period that von Manstein gained a deep and lasting respect for von Rundstedt's talent, learning many lessons which he would put to great use during the war years ahead.

Immediately following the immensely successful Polish campaign, Army Group A, under von Rundstedt, was transferred to the Western Front adjacent to the Belgium frontier where it prepared for the invasion of the West.

*See Guderian, Chapter 1.

The original German battle plan was almost an exact duplicate of the World War I "Schlieffen Plan," calling for a massive sweep through Holland and Belgium culminating in the envelopment and destruction of the French and British forces. Fortunately for Germany, a combination of factors forced a series of delays until suitable campaigning weather; for the year of 1939 had passed. These delays coupled with the fact that the original German plan fell into enemy hands necessitated a new and more original plan. This newer, bolder plan was subsequently put forward by its author, von Manstein.

After consultation with the great Panzer General, Heinz Guderian, von Manstein was convinced that Panzers could easily operate in the rugged terrain of the Ardennes Forest. He therefore proposed that the basic concept of the Schlieffen Plan be preserved in order to lure the enemy forces out of their fortifications while the main weight of the attack be shifted to the Ardennes where massed armour would roll up the Allied rear, cutting them off completely in a drive for the English Channel. This would enable the closely following infantry to squeeze the enemy between themselves and those forces striking south from the Lowlands.

The Berlin Generals, many of whom were old-fashioned in their thinking, took great pains to sweep this new plan under the rug while chastising its author. How dare a General in the field be so audacious as to question the working of the Army High Command. Manstein was to be relieved from his prestigious post and sent off to command an infantry corps. Even though this transfer entitled von Manstein to be promoted, the compliment was a backhanded one at best.

The Berlin Generals however, were not successful. At a reception for all recently promoted generals, Hitler, who was vaguely aware of von Manstein's plan, took the opportunity to have a private interview with the latter. Impressed with the General's intelligent assessment of the Allied capabilities and his obvious strategic talent, Hitler ordered a complete revision of the invasion plans based on von Manstein's ideas. The German leader had himself always been lukewarm to the Schlieffen concept and eagerly seized the opportunity to refute it. The adopted plan, the von Manstein plan as it is now known, proved to be highly successful, completely living up to its expectations and then some. By its implementation, Germany was able to easily conquer Holland, Belgium and France in the short span of six weeks, totally isolating Britain as well. The name von Manstein would not be lost to Hitler, this was assured.

In recognition of his achievement, von Manstein's corps was assigned the leading role for the forthcoming "Operation Sea Lion," the proposed invasion of England. With Sea Lion never becoming a reality, Manstein once again was shifted in command. His transfer to the Eastern Front culminated in the achievement of a treasured ambition; command of a Panzer Corps, the LVI. This Panzer Corps was one of two com-

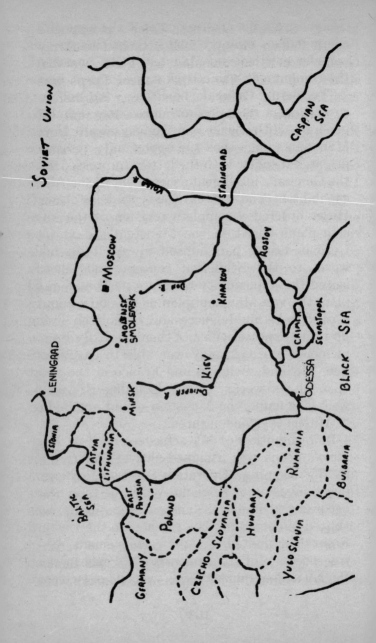

prising Colonel General Erich Hoeppner's Fourth Panzer Group, itself attached to Army Group North, commanded by Field Marshal Ritter von Leeb. The other Panzer Corps was commanded by General Hans Georg Reinhardt.

"Operation Barbarossa," the invasion of Russia, called for a three pronged assault: from the North towards Leningrad, the center towards Moscow, and the South into the Ukraine.

On June 22, 1941, the entire Eastern Front erupted in a hail of fire and steel. Von Manstein realized that Barbarossa was a great gamble and that its success depended upon the Germans knocking the Russians out during the first weeks of the attack. The only way to achieve this was to conquer and destroy the military and political centers of the country.

On the first day alone, LVI Panzer Corps advanced over fifty miles through a wide gap in the Russian defenses. By the 24th, von Manstein's troops found themselves over one hundred miles deep into Russian held territory after having cut the Dvinsk highway, their first objective. On June 26, von Manstein's Panzers captured the city of Dvinsk and the bridge over the Dvina River at Wilkomierze. But, permission to continue was denied by Hoeppner because the flanks of LVI Corps were not secure due to the slower advance of Reinhardt.

Von Manstein implored Hoeppner to reconsider, for he held the firm belief that his flanks were not vulnerable as long as the Panzers were

169

on the move and retained their mobility. He argued that by stopping, it invited static warfare that was totally unsuitable for tanks. However, the only concession gained was permission to enlarge the bridgehead and await the arrival of support.

Shortly thereafter, von Manstein's worst fears were realized when the Russians threw in strong counterattacks against the bridgehead that were beaten off only with the greatest difficulty. Finally, on July 2, permission to press on was received, but by now the Soviets had regrouped and greater opposition was to be expected. His new orders called for him to advance and sever communications between Moscow and Leningrad.

Progress was slow, the Soviets were desperately and fanatically resisting, applying strong pressure on the slow moving flanks and rear of LVI Panzer Corps. Nevertheless, by July 18, von Manstein had the situation well in hand. This nasty experience convinced von Manstein that the Panzer Group should consolidate for a strong drive on Leningrad. Early in August however, Hitler switched his primary objective from Moscow to Leningrad. The forces of von Manstein and Reinhardt were therefore directed to join hands for a drive on that city. At the same time, Guderian was diverted from Moscow to assist Army Group South's drive into the Ukraine.

Before LVI Panzer Corps could link up with Reinhardt for the drive on Leningrad, Soviet

General Vorisholov mounted a powerful counterattack against Busch's Eighteenth Army near Lake Ilmen. Von Manstein was pulled out of line and dispatched to the rescue where, after a headlong thrust, he rolled up the flank of the Russian Thirty Fourth Army, saving Busch from an embarrassing setback.

On September 12, von Manstein received a call from General Busch informing him of his new promotion. As Manstein himself recalls:

"On the evening of 12 September, under a steady downpour of rain, I was sitting in my tent with one or two officers of my staff. Ever since it had begun to get dark early we had taken to playing bridge to while away the time until evening situation reports came in. Suddenly the telephone rang at my elbow and I was asked to take a call from my friend Busch, the army commander. A telephone message at this late hour did not usually bode anything pleasant, on this occasion Busch read me out an order that had come over the telephone from O.K.H., "General of the Infantry von Manstein will leave forthwith for South Army Group to assume command of the Eleventh Army."[1]

Eleventh Army's objectives were twofold. They were to capture both the Crimea and Rostov. The latter held the highest priority since it was the gateway to the Caucasus whose oil fields contained all the oil the Germans could ever hope to possess.

Upon assuming command on September 17, von Manstein immediately realized that the task assigned his forces was too ambitious and would be physically impossible to accomplish without armour, none of which was available. Without this critical component, the dual objectives, physically separated by many miles, could not be attacked simultaneously. Eleventh Army was simply not capable of sustaining a dual offensive of this nature. Therefore, a decision as to which objective was to receive priority was required.

The Crimea seemed on the surface to be the most critical of the two. Russian air bases there posed a threat to the Rumanian oil fields and troops stationed on the Peninsula were a potential menace to the southern flank of Eleventh Army. In the hands of the Germans however, not only would these threats be eliminated, but a jumping off place into the Caucasus across the Kuban Isthmus could be secured. Von Manstein recognized the potential immediately and began drawing up plans for the conquest of the Crimea.

Fierce fighting marked the end of September and early October as the Soviets sensed the desperate situation that could arise should the Germans assault the Crimea. Two entire Soviet Armies attacked the Rumanian held position adjacent to the Eleventh Army. The Rumanians gave way easily and the Russians, with the momentum now in their hands, threatened to inflict a major disaster on the Eleventh Army by cutting the latter off with its back to the Black Sea.

After the great Kiev encirclement at the end of September, Kleist's First Panzer Army had been freed for other operations. Therefore, Kleist spearheaded a drive down the Dniepr River deep into the Russian rear. By October 5, the pendulum had swung the other way and within 5 days, the threat to Eleventh Army was eliminated.

The Rostov objective was now handed to Kleist, allowing Eleventh Army to concentrate solely on the Crimea. Months of fighting lay ahead for the German and Soviet forces on this historic Peninsula. Von Manstein rightly assumed that the Russians would attempt to regroup in their last Black Sea port, Sevastopol, and there attempt to hold out. As a result, von Manstein directed LIV and XXX Corps in the direction of this city while ordering XVII Corps westwards towards Kerch to prevent the Russians from fortifying the other objective of the Crimean campaign. On November 15, Kerch fell, denying the Russians an exit from the Crimea at that point. On the same day, the remainder of the Eleventh Army captured Balaclava, famous for the Charge of the Light Brigade at another time in a different war. Sevastapol then became the last holdout of Soviet resistance.

Faced with assaulting one of the most heavily fortified and defended positions in the world, Eleventh Army settled down for the siege and the bitter fighting that would undoubtedly accompany it. On December 17, the attack on Sevastapol began in earnest with General von

Richtofen's VIII Air Corps unleashing a devastating bombing attack on the defenses. With fierce hand to hand combat reminiscent of World War I, the Germans made slow progress but moved forward nonetheless. Once more however, the Russians were to thwart von Manstein's best laid plans by attacking across the frozen Kerch Strait from Taman on December 25. This attack posed a dire threat to the rear of Eleventh Army positioned at Sevastapol and was a situation that von Manstein could not ignore. Unable to stop the Soviet advance, he was therefore compelled to disengage his forces from the Sevastapol front and race to the threatened area.

By mid-January, Eleventh Army, reinforced by 2nd Panzer Division, managed to beat off the determined Soviet attack and stabilize the situation. But the severe winter conditions and the losses incurred in the fighting convinced von Manstein that it would be prudent to wait until spring before resuming the offensive.

The Russians used the winter lull to reinforce Sevastapol and the Kerch Peninsula, waiting for the expected onslaught with the advent of good weather. Early in May, Eleventh Army resumed the offensive on the Kerch front, knifing deep into the Russian flanks. In a brilliantly executed operation, von Manstein succeeded in destroying the Soviet Armies around Kerch. Once again, he found himself able to concentrate on Sevastapol.

On June 7, a tremendous artillery barrage heralded the renewed assault on the city. Bitter fighting marked every foot of the way. By July 1, the Russian positions had been compressed into the city proper. Three days later, the fortress of Sevastapol fell to the Germans along with over ninety thousand prisoners and a great deal of booty.

Von Manstein was suitably rewarded. The grateful Hitler ordered the creation of a special decoration to be awarded to all who fought in the Crimea. In addition, von Manstein was presented with the coveted baton symbolizing his promotion to the rank of Field Marshal. He had achieved what could be rightly considered the pinnacle of success for a soldier.

With the Crimea securely in German hands, the Wermacht began regrouping all along the front for the forthcoming 1942 Summer offensive. The most significant changes in the command structure took place in Army Group South. Field Marshal von Rundstedt, Army Group South's original commander-in-chief, had disagreed with Hitler the previous December over operations around Rostov. He was subsequently relieved of command and replaced by Field Marshal von Reichenau, a devoted and ardent Nazi. The latter too, agreed with his predecessor's goals and wound up carrying out the same plans that had resulted in von Rundstedt's being sacked. On January 17, Reichenau suffered a fatal stroke, dying a few days later. He was in turn replaced by Field Marshal von Bock, late commander of Army Group Center during the opening days of Barbarossa. Bock

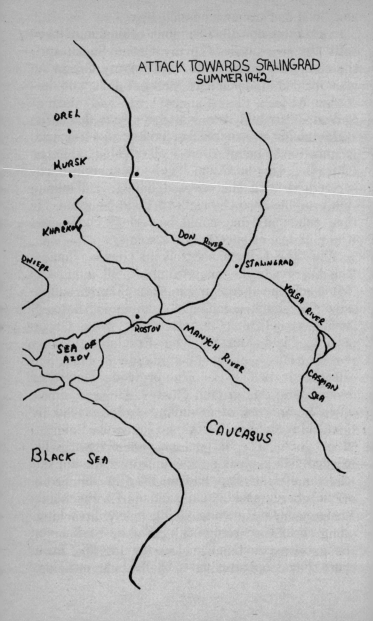

ATTACK TOWARDS STALINGRAD
SUMMER 1942

OREL

KURSK

KHARKOV

DNIEPR

DON RIVER

STALINGRAD

VOLGA RIVER

ROSTOV

MANYCH RIVER

SEA OF AZOV

CASPIAN SEA

CAUCASUS

BLACK SEA

had been in Germany on sick leave.

In planning the 1942 Summer offensive, Hitler split the objectives of Army Group South and the command structure as well. Army Group A was formed under Field Marshal List and included Kleist's First Panzer Army and Ruoff's Seventeenth Army along with various attached Italian units. Their objective was to clear the Donets Basin before driving Southwest into the Caucasus. Bock's Army Group B was comprised of Sixth Army under von Paulus, Fourth Panzer Army under General Hoth and the remainder of the Axis formations consisting of Italians, Rumanians and Hungarians. Bock's assignment was to clear the Don bend and drive to the Volga.

Hitler, blinded by the belief that the Russians were finished, and confident of victory, deleted von Manstein's Eleventh Army which was poised to strike from the Kerch Strait and sent this army instead to the Leningrad front, an order which von Manstein highly disagreed with.

At the end of June, the German Summer offensive began. At first, the assault resembled the massive offensives of the first year in Russia. With the vast open plains between the great Russian rivers being ideally suited for tanks, Kleist and Hoth made rapid headway and tore off huge chunks of Russian territory. First Panzer Army and Seventeenth Army, attacking along the lower Donets, prepared to blow open the gateway to the Caucasus at Rostov, from there they could advance to the Russian oilfields, a prize so highly coveted in Berlin.

Hoth, the commander of Fourth Panzer Army was assigned the task of protecting First Panzer Army's rear while advancing due East. Wheeling down the lower Don, Fourth Panzer Army knocked aside all opposition with relative ease and by early July was approaching Stalingrad, the great Soviet industrial city on the lower Volga, situated on the great Volga bend where that river took a sharp turn West to approach the Don River which bent Eastward at almost the same latitude.

Meanwhile, Kleist found himself bogged down before Rostov. Hitler, impatient for movement, ordered Hoth to wheel about 180 degrees and assist First Panzer Army. The German leader however, failed to take into consideration the nature of the Russian road system when issuing the order. The primitive roads in agricultural Russia were hard pressed to support a regular modern army let alone two entire Panzer Armies. With the confusion engendered by the mingling of Kleist's and Hoth's commands, the former politely informed Hitler that Hoth should proceed to his original objective. "He could do very well without additional help, thank you." Once more, the intrepid Hermann Hoth swung his army around and proceeded up the lower Don.

Meanwhile, Hitler began to focus greedily on the city of Stalingrad. Possessing some strategic importance, Stalingrad became by accident, partly by design, the focal point of the campaign. Its factories made it a distinct war asset, containing chemical and metallurgical works, railroads, and oil tank farms. Furthermore, its commanding position on the lower Volga River, the chief waterway of central Russia and the primary route for shipment of oil from the Caucasus, combined with its other industries, made Stalingrad a viable military objective for the Wermacht.

However, overconfidence began to dominate the German minds. Unlike the earlier successful campaigns, no huge bags of prisoners were being taken, a foreboding indicator of things to come. The Russians had obviously learned a bitter lesson and were no longer electing to stand and fight. When faced with overwhelming superiority, Stalin was now allowing his troops to fall back to positions in the rear, avoiding the huge encirclements typical of the previous year's conflict.

Bock was now superseded by Field Marshal von Weichs as commander of Army Group B. The new commander, responsible for co-ordinating the efforts of no less than seven armies, four of them allied, found the command arrangement too unwieldy, but his protestations fell on deaf ears. The highly overconfident Germans failed to recognize the signs.

After crossing the Don on August 18, Paulus, with orders to take Stalingrad, set out with his Sixth Army towards his objective. This order contradicted one of the cardinal rules that had made the German Army such a successful fighting machine. Sixth Army was, exclusive of

Fourth Panzer Army, Army Group B's most powerful striking force. Now it was given an objective that would reduce it to street fighting where loss of mobility would naturally dilute the strength of the German fighting force.

For flank cover, Paulus was required to rely on Third and Fourth Rumanian Armies, troops that were hardly the equal of the highly skilled, battle hardened Wermacht veterans. Poised far out on the steppe at Stalingrad, Sixth Army could hardly have felt secure in the face of bitter resistance. But their eyes were focused in one direction: forward.

On August 8th, IV Panzer Corps reached the Volga north of Stalingrad, but its commander, General Hans Hube decided not to enter the city until proper support could be brought up. By September, Sixth Army had linked up with Fourth Panzer Army operating south of the city and the assaulting of the city proper had begun. As was anticipated, street fighting bogged down the Germans and stripped the Panzers of their most prominent weapon, mobility. In addition, Paulus was beginning to run short of critical supplies and replacements. The Germans, in their haste to force a decision, had secured only one bridgehead over the Don, the bridge at Kalach. Through this bottleneck was forced to flow virtually all the supplies destined for the formations fighting east of the Don.

On November 9, 1942, Jodl handed Hitler the latest reports. "They indicated that the Russians were deploying not only northwest of Stal-

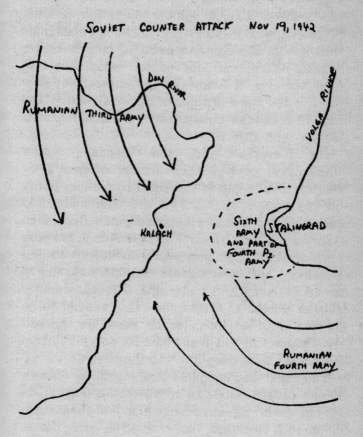

SOVIET COUNTER ATTACK   NOV 19, 1942

RUMANIAN THIRD ARMY

DON RIVER

VOLGA RIVER

KALACH

SIXTH ARMY AND PART OF FOURTH PZ. ARMY

STALINGRAD

RUMANIAN FOURTH ARMY

ingrad on the middle Don, opposite the Rumanian Third Army, but also south of the hotly contested city where two corps of the Rumanian Fourth Army were covering the flank of Hoth's Fourth Panzer Army."[2] All signs seemed to point to a Russian pincer operation against Sixth Army. Berlin however, although conscious that it was the Russian habit to launch winter counter-offensives, believed the main threat to be in the area of Army Group Center. They simply ignored the warnings of Army Group B and held firm in their conviction of a Russian attack on the central front.

On November 19, the Russians under Vasilezsky, opened their winter offensive by tearing a huge gap in the Third Rumanian Army on the upper Don. Before the Germans could react, Soviet troops attacked Fourth Rumanian Army and part of Fourth Panzer Army, blowing open another huge gap south of Stalingrad and knocking the unfortunate Rumanians and a great deal of Hoth's strength into the rapidly closing pocket of Stalingrad. This proved to be most costly to Hoth, for he was also charged with protecting the rear of Kleist's Army Group A, at this time deep into the Caucasus.

The rapid and complete disintegration of both flanks caused Hitler to admit that a deep crisis was in the offing. In order to alleviate the critical command situation, he created a new force, Army Group Don, which included both Rumanian Armies, Sixth Army and Fourth Panzer Army. Now, who could he turn to for leadership of

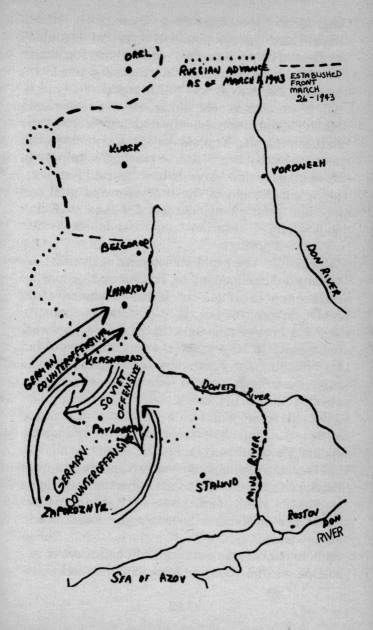

this force. He needed a man who could straighten out this potentially catastrophic situation. There was only one obvious choice. The only person capable of reversing the German fortunes was Erich von Manstein.

On November 20, the formal order was drafted and von Manstein set off once again for the Southern Front. Transportation as it was, he was reluctantly compelled to travel by train and it would be a few days before he could arrive. Taking advantage of the time afforded him, he and his staff kept abreast of the rapidly deteriorating situation and began devising countermeasures.

Meanwhile, the rapid Russian drive closed the ring around Sixth Army by linking up at Kalach. Weichs and Seydlitz, the latter commander of LVII Corps, part of Sixth Army, began clamoring for a breakout before the Russians had the opportunity to strengthen the ring. In answer to this pleading, the bombastic Goering convinced Hitler that Sixth Armies requirements could be satisfied via airlift conducted by his vaunted Luftwaffe. His boasting was refuted the next day by the Luftwaffe commander on the spot, Colonel General von Richtofen, to no avail. If Goering had shown more concern for the men at Stalingrad rather than his art collection, perhaps his hasty boast might not have been made. Nevertheless, Hitler acceded to the Reich Marshal's wishes.

By November 26, von Manstein had arrived on the Don and was busy familiarizing himself with the situation. In a communication with Hitler, he outlined the position and suggested alternatives. Hitler however, was adamant in affirming that a breakout was totally out of the question. Von Manstein refused to become discouraged. He was a pragmatic man, who had the ability to see beyond the immediate solution. Yes, Sixth Army was trapped, but far more was at stake than the fate of Sixth Army. The disposition of the entire German Southern wing invited a far more devastating fate than the loss of one army. As Manstein stated:

"The enemy would in the first instance do everything in his power to destroy the encircled Sixth Army. At the same time, we had to bear in mind the possibility that he would try to exploit the collapse of Third Rumanian Army by pushing mechanized forces across the large bend of the Don towards Rostov, where he was offered the prospect of cutting off the rear communications not only of Sixth and Fourth Panzer Army, but also of Army Group A."[3]

Those seven Soviet armies encircling Stalingrad would, if freed, pour down the Don valley like a tidal wave, creating a situation more dangerous than Stalingrad: 'a super-Stalingrad.' If Sixth Army were to be extradited, it had to be brought out intact and it must continue to tie down those armies now encircling it. Thus it was Army Group A in the Caucasus on whom von

Manstein focused his concern. This threat dominated the strategy.

Remnants of the Rumanian and German reinforcements were regrouped and placed opposite the Russian bridgehead at Kalach. Von Manstein then requested the withdrawal of Army Group A from the Caucasus, but permission for the latter was categorically denied by Hitler. The new commander of Army Group Don then requested at least a withdrawal of First Panzer Army in the Caucasus, now commanded by General von Mackensen with Kleist having moved up to Army Group Command. Von Manstein argued that this army would be essential to stem the Russian tide. Once again, permission was emphatically denied.

Meanwhile, deterioration of the situation at Stalingrad was rapidly approaching the critical stage. Although morale had risen slightly when the troops learned of von Manstein's presence on the Southern front, the Russian stranglehold was thickening the noose and Goering's idle boasts could not be made good. Even the basic minimum of supplies could not be ferried into the pocket. Yet, von Manstein was not fully convinced of the need for Sixth Army to break out. He wanted to exhaust all possible alternatives before yielding the initiative. Nevertheless, a plan was drafted for a relief operation designed to cut a corridor through to Paulus beleaguered force. If successful, Sixth Army might be sustained or, in the event this proved too costly, the route for a breakout would at least exist.

When a workable plan was agreed on by von Manstein and his staff, Paulus was informed of the role Sixth Army was to play in the relief operation. The plan called for a reinforced Fourth Panzer Army to attack up the lower Volga in the direction of Stalingrad. When the attacking forces reached a point approximately thirty miles south of the city, Paulus was to launch a counterstroke in the opposite direction and link up with Hoth. Meanwhile, a second attack from the West would serve to keep the Russians from concentrating against Hoth's spearheads. Paulus, however, replied that he had enough fuel available for only a twenty mile advance and doubted he could mount enough strength to break through the Russian ring anyway. In effect, he was attempting to avoid responsibility for a breakout by insisting that Hoth traverse the entire distance into Stalingrad. This put a real deterrent on von Manstein's plans and gave him an inclination of Paulus' peculiar brand of military logic.

Nevertheless, Army Group Don command was determined to move ahead with the operation despite Paulus's reluctance to cooperate. The operation was called "Winterstorm." Although unable to obtain permission from Berlin to withdraw Kleist, von Manstein at least succeeded in having I Panzer Corps transferred from Mackensen's command to reinforce Hoth. The planned assault was to be launched on December 8.

The Russians however, had no intention of easing the pressure and making things easy for the Germans. For the Soviets, the Chir River line was most important. Pressure on the Chir not only could lead to the breakthrough to Rostov and all that it entailed, but it would also cause the Germans to drain their strength from other sectors. That is exactly what transpired. Von Manstein was forced to withdraw units from Hoth in an effort to ease the Russian pressure. In addition, the troops intended for the attack from the west of Stalingrad in conjunction with Hoth's attack, had to be used in a defensive role and were of no help at all to Fourth Panzer Army.

Nevertheless, a much weakened Fourth Panzer Army launched the offensive on December 12 in the direction of Stalingrad. Despite firm Soviet resistance and severe cold, initial progress was good and by December 19, the Germans had reached a point forty five miles from the pocket. The attack soon became bogged down however in the face of heavy Russian opposition and increased pressure on the Rumanians guarding the flank of the advance. Hoth was not only saddled with the responsibility for relieving Stalingrad, but the protection of Rostov was his as well. At all costs, the escape route for Army Group A must be held open.

Therefore, he was required to pay close attention to the situation on his flanks and in his rear.

With Hoth reasonably close to Stalingrad, von Manstein now attempted to have Paulus shoulder his share of the responsibility. The latter was queried as to the possibility of linking up with Hoth via an attack southward. Sixth Army's commander replied that the fuel available was enough for only an eighteen mile advance. In addition, Paulus wanted assurances that Hitler approved of a withdrawal from Stalingrad. Von Manstein could have ordered Paulus out to link up with Hoth but by overruling Hitler, he would find himself out of a job and he was still firmly convinced that he could salvage the situation and was therefore not prepared to relinquish his command. In retrospect, although it may resemble an egotistical and arrogant way of thinking, it was however a cold, hard fact. Von Manstein was the only commander available with enough strategical ability to stem the tide.

It was at this time, on December 16, that the Russians unleashed their offensive against the Italian Eighth Army on the Chir. Numerous Russian armoured and infantry formations crashed through the Italian front and opened a gap one hundred miles wide between Army Group Don and Army Group B, through which they poured southwards towards Rostov. Von Manstein was compelled to transfer forces from the Stalingrad operation to fill the gap, for a cataclysmic situation was in the making with the lives of more than a million men at stake.

With Army Group Don forced to denude the already weakened Fourth Panzer Army, responsibility now fell on Paulus to assume the initiative or forfeit any chance for relief. Incredibly, he still refused to act, thereby sealing the fate of Sixth Army.

The increased pressure on his left flank no longer afforded von Manstein the luxury of a wide dispersal of his forces. He therefore, regrouped the remnants of the Italian, Rumanian, and German support groups along with the reinforcements from Hoth into a detachment under General Karl Hollidt. This force was positioned directly in the path of the onrushing Russians and managed to slow down, but not stop, the advancing Soviet horde. The creation of Army Detachment Hollidt ended Hoth's hope of relieving Stalingrad. However, Hoth was a pragmatist and realized the situation boiled down to a choice between a greater or lesser disaster.

Increased Russian pressure forced Hoth to withdraw step by step in an effort to avoid encirclement of his own troops. Help was desperately required. Von Manstein was besieging Hitler with requests for Army Group A's evacuation from the Caucasus. The latter was still reluctant to relinquish already conquered territory and avoided making a firm decision. Fourth Panzer Army was the only force available to protect the rear of Army Group A and, should it be unable to hold Rostov, two additional German armies would be doomed.

By the end of December, the fate of Stalingrad was virtually sealed. Von Manstein had correctly diagnosed the Russian intentions. The Soviets were intent on the total destruction of Sixth Army in a fixed battle of annihilation rather than leaving them to wither on the vine. This suited von Manstein just fine, for, by its mere existence alone, Sixth Army was tying down huge concentrations of enemy troops that would, if released, wreak havoc on the rest of Army Group Don and if successful, cut off the whole of Army Group A. Although no one cared to admit it, Sixth Army was being written off as a total loss whose only contribution to their comrades would be the tying down of the Soviet Army in order to forestall its drive on Rostov.

Meanwhile, back at the Wolf's Lair, Hitler was rapidly awakening to the danger on the Southern front. With both of Hollidt's flanks now in jeopardy, he reluctantly gave his consent for a strategic withdrawal of all forces above Stalingrad. Taking immediate advantage of the temporary relaxation of the stand fast order, von Manstein ordered Hollidt and the Fretter-Pico detachment further north to retreat to the Donets River and construct a defensive line at that point. During the first week of the year, Hollidt, using his meager Panzer reinforcements to blunt the Russian spearheads, began his retreat to the Donets. Two weeks later, both Army Detachments reached this line and began to dig in.

The Don Front was not the only scene of Russian pressure. Hoth's weakened Fourth Panzer Army was steadily being driven back in the face of increased Red Army activity. To avoid encirclement, Hoth was forced back step by step, retreating river by river; Sal, Kuberle, Manych, thus increasing the already considerable distance between Fourth Panzer Army and Sixth Army. Finally, by January 19, Hoth had managed to link up with First Panzer Army on the Manych Canal where these units were able to form a cohesive front. The escape route for Army Group A was still being held open.

While Hoth, Fretter-Pico and Hollidt were beating a retreat, the Russians once more struck. This time against the Hungarians holding the area between the Don and Weich's Army Group B. By the end of the 3rd week in January, Army Group B's front was torn open on a two hundred mile stretch. Weichs reported to Hitler that he saw no way to stem the tide.

Von Manstein monitered the events on the upper Don with a feeling of deep frustration. Forced to protect Kleist's rear, he was powerless to come to the aid of the Hungarian Second Army. In addition, the Russian breakthrough was driving down the left flank of Army Group Don.

Kleist meanwhile, had himself formally requested permission to evacuate his army from the Caucasus while Rostov was still in German hands. Von Manstein praised Army Detachment Hollidt for its ability in holding the exit open:

"The fact that the Army Detachment succeeded in finally halting the enemy on the Donets and thereby saving Fourth Panzer Army and Army Group A from being cut off south of the Don, must be ascribed first and foremost. While not forgetting the way its

192

staff handled operations—to the bravery with which the infantry divisions and all other formations and units helping to hold the line stood their ground against the enemy's recurrent attacks."[4]

Even though Hollidt was doing his best in holding open the exit, Kleist stated that further delay would result in disaster. Hitler hedged, but on January 27, 1943, ordered First Panzer Army transferred from Kleist's command to Army Group Don. By now, Rostov was untenable and, with most of Army Group A withdrawn into the Taman bridgehead with the First Panzer Army evacuated through Rostov, it was time for the Germans to reach a decision.

At Kharkov, General Lanz's Army Detachment had just received the command of a relatively strong Panzer Corps under S.S. General Paul Hausser. Von Manstein's plan called for this corps to attack the Russian flank. However, Hitler was not in favor of this attack, for he insisted on holding on to Kharkov at all costs. Nevertheless, von Manstein persisted, and on February 3, Hitler authorized the attack. It was too little, too late. On February 2, Stalingrad finally fell to the Russians. With the subsequent increase in strength of the latter, the German attack failed when it was finally launched a week later.

On February 6, 1943, von Manstein flew to Hitler's Headquarters to discuss the situation. What von Manstein desired was the evacuation of the Donets line and a withdrawal to the Mius. He had come intending to propose this strategy and to propose that Hitler lay down the active command and appoint a qualified professional. However, "When the two met, Hitler, with no preliminaries, declared that he accepted sole responsibility for the debacle at Stalingrad."[5] This unnerved von Manstein, for it was quite unexpected. Turning from the topic of command to that of the front, von Manstein demonstrated to Hitler in detail that retreat to the Mius River was imperative. The latter retorted that shortening the line would release as many Russian troops as German and furthermore, Germany could ill afford the loss of the coal in the Donets basin. After debating for over four hours, Hitler reluctantly gave his permission to withdraw to the Mius.

On February 8, Army Detachment Hollidt took the first backward step to the Mius. Together with Fourth Panzer Army, it covered the 100 mile distance in nine days. Another decision reached at the aforementioned conference cost Weich's command of Army Group B. That Army Group was dissolved with the remnants of the Hungarian Second Army assigned to Army Group Center and the balance, primarily the shattered Allied formations, handed over to Army Group Don.

With von Manstein preoccupied with the evacuation to the Mius, the highly logical SS General Hausser began demanding the evacuation of Kharkov. However, his immediate superior, Wermacht General Lanz, refused permission and demanded adherence to Hitler's order, since the latter insisted that Kharkov must not be lost, but instead be held as a fortress. Was another Stalingrad in the offing? Hausser however, was a more formidable character than Paulus and threatened to pull his troops out regardless. In frustration, Lanz reluctantly gave his consent for a complete evacuation and was subsequently sacked by Hitler. However, by retreating from Kharkov, Hausser had saved his Corps and these fanatic and hard fighting troops were to prove a welcome addition to Army Group Don.

With Army Detachment Hollidt back on the Mius and First Panzer Army under Mackensen rotated to the threatened northern wing of the Army Group on the middle Donets, Hoth's Fourth Panzer Army was moved from the lower Don through snow and slush, to the area between the Donets and the Dnieper bend on the western wing of the Army Group. A few sentences could not describe the horror and confusion of moving such vast amounts of men and machines.

"The roads were covered with deep snow. The drivers were overtired. There were endless traffic jams. There were accidents, the columns were strung out over great distances. The engineers got no sleep at all. Time and again, the divisional commanders toured their regiments, urging them on, reminding them of the dangers, imploring them forward, forward![6]

Von Manstein moved his headquarters from Stalino to Zaporozhye and his Army Group was renamed. On February 14, it was designated Army Group South.

With Kharkov now in Soviet hands, it appeared to the Soviets that the entire annihilation of Hitler's southern wing was imminent. Von Manstein recognized the Soviet intention of cutting off the three German Armies and two Army Detachments. He sensed that the optimism in the Russian camp might be used against them. The Soviets were convinced that the Germans were in full retreat and had obvious proof of this; the retreat of an SS Panzer Corps from Kharkov. A Stavka order to the South-West Front demanded: "You are to prevent the enemy's withdrawal to Dnepropetrovsk and Zaporozhye, throw back the enemy forces into the Crimea, block the approaches to the Crimea, and thus cut off the German southern group."[7] Von Manstein was watching the Soviets, awaiting his opportunity. The Red Army continued to advance, convinced by their double-agents, particularly a "Man Called Lucy" that the Germans were in full retreat. This added to the Soviet optimism. However, they did not reckon with a man of von Manstein's caliber.

On February 17, Hitler arrived at the headquarters of Army Group Don where the Field Marshal unfolded his plan to the Fuhrer. Hitler was excited and nervous but he sensed, "that it was not he who was weaving the pattern, but that outstanding strategic brain which, as long ago as 1940 as Chief of Staff of Army Group A, had worked out the formula for victory in the French campaign."[8] Now von Manstein was formulating yet another brilliant plan. Reporting the situation to Hitler, he related that Army Detachment Hollidt had successfully established itself on the Mius and was resisting strong attacks by three Soviet armies. General Mackensen's First Panzer Army adjoining Hollidt on the left was succeeding in intercepting attacks by units of the Soviet First Guards Army but a wide gap still remained between it and Army Detachment Lanz, now renamed Kempf since Lanz's sacking after Hausser's evacuation of Kharkov. Into this huge gap the Soviet thrust was aimed, and it was here that von Manstein hoped to perform the miracle that would save the German Army from complete collapse.

On the night of February 18, Headquarters, Fourth Panzer Army under Hoth arrived in Zaporozhye, site of von Manstein's headquarters. There, the commander of Army Group South outlined Fourth Panzer Army's mission orally to Hoth. He told him that he intended to put a new, reinforced Fourth Panzer Army in the gap between Kempf and Mackensen. Hoth's first assignment would be to stop the Soviet First Guards and Sixth Armies east of Dnepropetrovsk and throw them back across the Samara River.

197

Before leaving Zaporozhye, Hitler, on February 19, called the commander of Army Group A, Kleist, and directed him to evacuate as many of his troops as possible from the Taman bridgehead and transfer them to Army Group South.

The Germans, being reinforced with more troops and better and more air power, were ready; all that remained was for the Soviets to move into the trap. Just at that point the Soviet offensive was renewed with a major thrust into the gap between First Panzer Army and Army Detachment Kempf. They approached to within forty miles of the Dnieper and a mere sixty miles from Zaporozhye. Hitler, still present, became quite nervous over the situation. One of the many reasons for his visit to von Manstein's headquarters was the intention of sacking the latter, but now there was no other alternative but to give the green light for the counteroffensive. Even at that, Hitler became jittery and was ready to water down von Manstein's plan. A Soviet combat group commander unwittingly put an end to Hitler's interference when, on February 19, he thrust from Pavlograd to Sinelnikov, a mere forty miles from the headquarters of Army Group South. Between there and the Soviets stood not a single German unit. Hitler wisely decided to make a hasty departure, leaving von Manstein free to act. "The Field Marshal heaved a sigh of relief when his distinguished visitor disappeared in the grey wintry sky towards Vinnistsa. Now at last he had a free hand."[9]

It was time now for the Germans to strike. From France came the fresh 15th Infantry Division! They were immediately dispatched to Sinelnikov, going directly from their trains into battle, taking the Russians completely by surprise. Meanwhile, the two pincers for the main operation were assembling. The SS Panzer Corps under the astute Paul Hausser assembled around Krasnograd and the Fourth Panzer Army south-east of Pavlograd. By February 23, the advance guard of the Soviet Sixth Army was in a hopeless situation. In addition, the Popov Group was halted by the SS Viking Division north of Krasnoarmeyskoye. Popov pleaded with Stalin for permission to retreat, but all he received was a bland assurance that the Germans were in retreat and that he should continue the attack southward with vigour. Wheeling north, in a concerted motion, Hausser's SS Corps and the XLVIII Panzer Corps proceeded to slice the protruding neck of the Sixth Army into shreds while XL Panzer Corps was decimating Popov's command.

By February 27, the Germans were approaching the Donets in strength, with the Red Army falling back in disorder across the melting river. In a headlong offensive, Hoth's Panzers drove hard against the Russian formations, encircling them and smashing them completely. Trying to estimate what this loss meant to the Russians is difficult to state briefly.

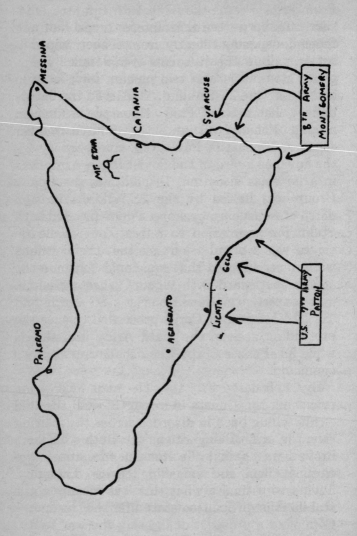

One author has tried to tabulate some of the costly figures.

"Six tank corps, ten rifle divisions, and half a dozen independent brigades had been wiped out or badly mauled. A total of 615 tanks, 400 guns, and 600 anti-tank guns had been destroyed, 23,000 Soviet dead littered the battlefield. The ratio of dead to wounded is normally put at one to five. That would mean an effective loss of 100,000 Russian troops."[10]

Von Manstein then sent the SS Panzer Corps in an arc west of the city of Kharkov and Fourth Panzer Army in an arc to the east between the city and the river. The SS Corps then wheeled through the city and once more raised the Swastika in Kharkov's Red Square. "Hausser had atoned for his disobedience, von Manstein was completely vindicated."[11]

On March 18, Belograd fell to the Germans before the spring thaw finally ended the campaign. Only a large salient around Kursk remained to the Soviets. The Germans were back on the Donets, the very position they held the previous spring. As von Manstein stated:

"By the end of the winter campaign the initiative was back in German hands, and the Russians had suffered two defeats. Though not decisive in character, these did lead to a stabilization of the front and offer the German Command a prospect of fighting the war to a draw.[12]

Thus, the German Army was given a new lease on life.

The great Bulge at Kursk still loomed as a threat to the gap between Army Groups Center and South, causing von Manstein to suggest a swift blow against it. Unfortunately for the Germans, wide disagreements by various top commanders caused repeated delays and when Operation Citadel was finally launched against the Kursk salient, the Russians held it in such force that it proved impossible to penetrate. By this time, because of the frequent delays, von Manstein himself was convinced of the futility of Citadel and his predictions of total failure proved disastrously accurate. The German Panzer forces were severely mauled at Kursk and were unable to recoup their losses. Once more the momentum swung to the Russians who were never to relinquish it.

After Kursk, the Eastern front became one German disaster after another with retreat following retreat. A new Russian offensive on the extreme Southern front was launched in August by no less than three Soviet Army Groups. Understrength, and with his lines stretched to the breaking point, von Manstein was unable to halt the Red Army surge. Kharkov fell for the fifth and final time as Army Group South was compelled to retreat to the Dnieper River.

The Soviets continued to maintain the pressure all along the front and this constant fighting finally forced von Manstein to order the evacuation of the Dnieper bend in mid December following the fall of Kiev. Seven German divisions were trapped by the Soviet advance in the Korsun Pocket on the lower Dnieper. Although von Manstein managed to open a narrow corridor into the pocket, he could only keep the escape route open for a few hours, resulting in heavy German loss of life.

Still the Russian attacks continued with the Germans being forced back step by step. In mid March, the Soviets managed to tear open a huge gap between First and Fourth Panzer Armies deep in the south. (Kleist's Army Group was, by now, facing North and in imminent danger of being totally cut off and destroyed.) Once again, von Manstein's gift for maneuver managed to stave off total destruction but his days in command were now numbered. After sacking general after general for withdrawing without concurrence, Hitler finally got around to von Manstein.

On March 30, 1944, Hitler dispatched an aircraft to von Manstein's headquarters to transport the Field Marshal to a conference at the former's headquarters. As he climbed aboard, von Manstein was greeted by Kleist who had also been summoned. Upon arrival at Hitler's headquarters, the two Field Marshals were notified of their relief. In von Manstein's own words:

"Saw the Fuhrer in the evening. After handing me the Swords to my Knight's Cross, he announced that he had decided to place the

Army Group in other hands. (Model's), as the time for grand-style operations in the east, for which I had been particularly qualified, was now past."[13]

Thus, the three most prominent figures in the fierce struggle for the Ukraine (Hoth had been relieved earlier) went off into retirement for the duration of the war.

How great was von Manstein? No less an authority than Liddell Hart has called him "The Allies most formidable opponent." His peers looked upon von Manstein with great respect; the fact that they tried many times to convince Hitler to appoint von Manstein Commander-in-Chief of the Army attest to this. The French campaign surpassed even the highest hope of the German Army. The Crimean campaign was a brilliantly conducted masterpiece. However, the post-Stalingrad campaign was probably the most outstanding feat of arms of the entire war and one of the greatest demonstrations of recovery in military history. Brilliant in concept and superbly orchestrated by a masterful commander with a keen sense of strategy and tactics, the restoration of the German forces culminated in their holding virtually the same lines as those held the previous summer. This after the colossal disaster at Stalingrad.

Although post-war notoriety similar to that of a Rommel or Guderian eluded him, it is von Manstein's name that history will rank with those of Alexander the Great, Hannibal, Napoleon and Lee.

Field Marshal Albert Kesselring

Chapter 5

Albert Kesselring, along with Erwin Rommel, Heinz Guderian and Erich von Manstein must be considered one of the finest and most prominent and successful German commanders of World War II. Though not as well known as the others, his tasks and responsibilities in many ways, completely surpassed them.

Among his achievements during a long military career was the laying of the foundation stone for the Luftwaffe. It was he who shook the British during the Battle of Britain and who directed the destruction of the Russian Air Force during the early days of Operation Barbarossa. It was Kesselring who was sent to restore order out of the chaos that marked the Mediterranean Theatre at the end of 1941, matching wits with a talented, but ambitious and glory seeking commander, Erwin Rommel, and embroiling himself in the all too sticky political situations involved in coalition warfare. Again, it was this officer who saved the day after the Italian defection and who miraculously held the Allies for almost nine months before allowing the capture of Rome, which by that time proved so costly a contest that all prestige for the Allies was tarnished. Finally, it was Kesselring to whom Hitler turned in March 1945, to take over command of the Western Front after the capture of an intact bridge across the Rhine at Remagan.

S.L.A. Marshall has called Kesselring a multiple person because of the many tasks he performed during the war. He proved himself the master in both offensive and defensive warfare, but it was as the master of prolonged defensive warfare that Kesselring has few rivals in history. For a period of over two and one half years, he fought a virtually incessant delaying action against desperate odds, accomplishing what most of his superiors and many of his subordinates thought was impossible. It is this achievement that the authors intend to highlight as this commander's greatest accomplishment. The rest of his career will also be sketched, but it is his prolonged defensive tactics in Italy that finds Field Marshal Kesselring depicting the characteristics that make him stand out as one of the great commanders of the Second World War. Hitler too, eventually reached the same conclusion, for Kesselring was virtually the only Commander-in-Chief who, after 1941, managed to change Hitler's way and survive. He argued and won, and to prove this point, Kesselring was called upon by his leader in March, 1945, to salvage the Western Front.

Albert Kesselring was born on November 30, 1885 in Southern Germany. Though coming from a non-military family, his one ambition from the time he matriculated in grammar school in 1904, was to be a soldier. Not being the son of an officer, he could not enter the army as a cadet but rather was required to volunteer as an aspiring officer, hoping then to be nominated. He was finally nominated by the commanding officer of the 2nd Bavarian Foot Artillery Regiment.

From 1905 to 1906, he attended the Military Academy and from 1909-1910, the Artillery School. Most of his pre-World War I training was in and around the city of Metz where, amid the landscape of Lorraine, he revelled in the military glories that brought this land into German possession.

In 1911, he married Pauline Kayssler who remained his wife until her death. It was a marriage not filled with the hopes and desires of most young men, for it was loveless and childless.

When the First World War began, his regiment was already on the Western Front in occupation of the Western forts at Metz. During the war, he held many and varied staff positions. Except for one month that was spent on the Eastern Front in 1917, all his experience was in the West. He also received practical indoctrination into the essential principles of two key weapons of modern war: heavy artillery and air power. These became principles that he never forgot.

One of his commanders rated him as "extremely capable."[1] and because of his excellent record and reputation, he was recommended to the

General Staff, into which he was accepted in 1918.

His last assignment was to the II and III Bavarian Army Corps as a General Staff Officer. Here, he came into close contact with the humanitarian, Crown Prince Rupprecht of Bavaria. They shared many hours together in conversation ranging from art to statescraft and it was from Rupprecht that he learned the humanitarian principles that were evident in the conduct of all his campaigns during World War II.

Another personality whom Kesselring came into contact with at this time was General Hans von Seeckt. From this relationship, Kesselring learned the fine arts of organizing, negotiating, and manipulating. Thus, the humanity of Rupprecht and the talent of von Seeckt melded together to help form the personality of this aspiring commander.

With the end of the First World War and the accompanying horrors of civil strife in the wake of the demise of the autocracy and the birth of the democracy, Bavaria toyed with communism, leading to counterrevolution and the horrors of fratricide. Kesselring, observing this madness, indelibly marked in his mind the evils of communism and partisan warfare. Never would he forget these experiences.

Because of Seeckt's high esteem for him, Kesselring was chosen as one of the lucky 100,000 man army allowed by the punitive Treaty of Versailles. Central to Seeckt's problem was the building of this army with the latest technology and techniques.

Kesselring's first position in the new army was as Senior Staff Officer to the Chief of Staff of the Army Training Department. This position demanded frequent contact with air matters. Seeckt realized the importance of an air force in the new army and took steps to insure that his creation included former aviators. Such men as Hugo Sperrle, Kurt Student, Helmut Wilberg, Wilhelm Wimma and Hellmuth Felmy were on the rolls of the new army. Outlawed by Versailles, the new air force was conceived in secrecy and these men were selected to be the future leaders. But it was in two non-aviators that Seeckt detected the aptitudes for leadership in the fledgling air force: Walter Wever and Albert Kesselring.

Before Kesselring reached that position of leadership in the new Luftwaffe, Seeckt sought to give his protege as much staff experience as possible.

"Von Seeckt 'by shifting Kesselring from one task to another, dealing with all branches of training, technical problems, legal affairs' and matters of international importance, ensured that one of his most favoured younger proteges acquired an almost unique breadth of experience in as wide a variety of posts as possible within a five year span."[2]

By 1930, he had served in all the principal

staff branches, and his rank was advanced to full Colonel.

In 1933, Hitler came to power and riding his coattails as a close and trusted advisor came the former Luftwaffe Ace, Hermann Goering. Consequently, as the army grew, with it grew a strong air force thanks to Goering's influence. By September 1933, plans were sufficiently progressed to make the first senior appointments to the air arm. Colonel Stumpff asked Kesselring if he would be interested in the position of Administrative Director of the Luftwaffe with responsibility for budgeting, personnel, accommodation and construction. He was not fully happy, for he had hoped that the Luftwaffe would be part of the Army rather than a separate entity, but it had already been designated that it be separate and so Kesselring was required to formally resign from the Army to assume his position in the Luftwaffe. All procedures were carried out with the utmost secrecy, for an air force was still outlawed. Thus, Kesselring wore mufti to and from his office, the pretext being that he held a civilian position.

At the age of 48, he learned to fly, achieving a high level of proficiency. Proof of this came during the war when, on five separate occasions, his plane was shot down and each time he managed to bring the aircraft down safely.

The Luftwaffe was officially unveiled in 1935. Kesselring now found himself able to resume his military career in the open, taking at this time, as did all military personnel, the oath of allegiance to the Fuhrer, Adolf Hitler. An oath for Kesselring was a lifetime commitment, a fact that would be most forcefully observed during his wartime career.

Kesselring's feat in recruiting and training the cadres of the rapidly expanding Luftwaffe and of molding this organization, are amongst his greatest achievements. On August 15, 1936, he became Chief of Staff of the Luftwaffe after the untimely death of Wever. At that time, the Condor Legion was in Spain, where it was learning extremely valuable combat lessons.

In 1937, Kesselring violently disagreed with his superior, Erhard Milch, which led the former to request being relieved of his position as Chief of the General Staff of the Luftwaffe.

From the middle of 1937 until the latter days of September, 1938, he was in command of the III Air Region in Dresden. Then, on October 1, 1938, he became Chief of Staff of Luftflotte I in Berlin. Here Kesselring faced his first crisis, when the infant Luftwaffe was called upon to be ready to take offensive action against a potential enemy, Czechoslovakia. Accordingly, Kesselring welcomed the Munich conference which he saw as saving the Luftwaffe from suffering heavy combat sacrifices.

After the occupation of the balance of Czechoslovakia in March 1939, the Luftflotte I Chief often travelled from Berlin to Prague, inspecting the deployments of his fleet in the newly acquired Czech airdromes. Though dismayed by the turn of events and the collapse of the

Munich Agreements, he nevertheless completely accepted that his government was correct and was merely responding to acts of aggression attributed to the Czechs.

Kesselring watched the events of August, 1939, with keen interest. War was not desired by him, for war meant warfare in the air and the only experience the Luftwaffe had was during the Spanish Civil War. If war could be avoided, well then Kesselring would be overjoyed. If not, he of course stood ready to do his duty as a loyal German Officer.

September 1, 1939, ended any hope of a peaceful solution, as ground and air units struck the Polish armed forces a crippling blow. The main task of the Luftwaffe during the opening stages of the Polish campaign was to destroy all opposition from the Polish Air Force and to support the army and harass enemy strategic concentrations and troop movements.

The campaign fully demonstrated Kesselring's development as a leader and commander. He flew among his formations deep into hostile air space, including over Warsaw, in his attempts to assess the enemy's ability to resist and to evaluate his own men's performance, all the while, providing encouragement.

Luftflotte I was responsible for the northern section of the attack. The Germans held the initiative from the start and possessed superior weapons and logistics. The superb coordination between Kesselring's Luftflotte I and von Bock's Army Group regarding ground to air offensive tactics provided badly needed experience for future campaigns.

At the conclusion of the campaign in Poland, Kesselring was awarded the coveted Knight's Cross of the Iron Cross for his role. He then went home to his family for a rest, fully cognizant of the fact that France and England would be more formidable opponents for Germany.

Once his leave was over, he returned to Poland where he organized the air defenses and established a training base for new aircrews.

On January 10, 1940, an event occurred that had a far reaching effect on Kesselring's subsequent career. An airplane crashed over Belgium. In this plane were two officers carrying the complete plans for the invasion of the west. Hitler, furious over the fact that the French and British might have access to these plans as a result of this careless act, ordered Goering to punish those responsible. The incumbent commander of Luftflotte II was therefore transferred and Albert Kesselring was ordered by Goering to assume command, thereby thrusting him into a vital role for the forthcoming offensive.

How would the Luftwaffe perform in the West? Poland had fallen rapidly, but now Germany faced two powerful enemies, England and France. Kesselring could only hope that the Germans would prove superior and that the many valuable lessons learned in Poland would give them the edge necessary to defeat the French and British.

Kesselring's Luftflotte II was once more

assigned to support von Bock's command, Army Group B. He was quite content to work again with the latter since from their experience in Poland, they found that they worked extremely well together.

On May 10, 1940, the day the attack in the West began, Kesselring was directing General Kurt Student's air landing group whose critical assignment was to capture the bridges across the Albert Canal, the main bridges over the Maas, the airfields in Rotterdam and the impregnable Belgian fortress of Fort Eben Emael. Completely successful in these tasks and with the collapse of Holland and Belgium, his air fleet was now handed the task of annihilating the remains of the British Expeditionary Force which had retreated to the coastal town of Dunkirk.

Goering convinced Hitler that the Luftwaffe would accept sole responsibility for the destruction of the BEF, thus saving the German armour for the task of conquering metropolitan France. Kesselring tried in vain to convince Goering that after almost three weeks of ceaseless operations by his aircrews, the job simply could not be done. Many factors contributed to the escape of the British. Besides general fatigue experienced by the airmen, Kesselring credited the British Spitfire as the saviour of the British and French, along with poor weather and visibility which either grounded the Luftwaffe or made visibility so poor that hitting targets became difficult. The entire affair convinced Kesselring that air attacks, unless followed up by a determined ground assault, could not bring about victory. The coordination of both air and ground assault were necessary ingredients for total victory.

While the battle for the Dunkirk perimeter was in full sway, Kesselring observed with pride the German Army preparations for phase 2 of the Battle of France. From his personal plane, high over the assembly areas, he commented:

> "No one who saw from the air, as I did, von Kleist's and Guderian's armour veering round towards the Somme and the Aisne, after striking towards the Channel, could stifle a feeling of pride at the flexibility and skill of the German Command and fighting-fitness of the troops."[3]

Except for the successful evacuation of the BEF, Kesselring could boast of a tremendous victory for the Luftwaffe. With the subsequent collapse of the French and the signing of the armistice, the possibility of peace loomed large. Kesselring was naturally quite overjoyed by this prospect, but yet he took stock. The lessons of the Polish campaign had been put into practice with tremendous effect. He was extremely proud of the close cooperation achieved between Army Group B and Luftflotte II. Now the question remained, would the British continue the war?

There was some hope that an invasion of the British Isles would not be necessary. But, as the weeks went by, the hope dimmed. By the middle of July, the order to begin preparations for the air battle against England was received. Accordingly, Kesselring personally conducted air reconnaissance along the Channel coast.

On July 19, 1940, Hitler, during a speech to the Reichstag, promoted Kesselring to the coveted rank of Field Marshal. In the same speech, Hitler also included a peace message aimed at the British. In all sincerity, Kesselring accepted the message at face value and with hopes that the British would accept.

The Battle of Britain however, was inevitable. In his autobiography, Kesselring defends the conduct of the Luftwaffe and concludes that Germany did not seriously contemplate an invasion against the island. Though the Luftwaffe was thrown into the attack to destroy the RAF, thus paving the way for an invasion, in reality, it was an invasion that had not been seriously contemplated by the OKW*. Defending the Luftwaffe because of the blame placed on it for not bringing England to her knees, Kesselring states:

"Permanent air supremacy was impossible without the occupation of the island for the simple reason that a considerable number of British air bases, aircraft and engine factories were out of range of our bombers."[4]

If Kesselring had lived long enough, he would also have learned that his Enigma cihper

*German High Command.

messages, the very secret code which the Germans believed unbreakable, were being read by the British, allowing Hugh Dowding, the commander of the British Fighter Command, to foil Kesselring's attempts to bring the RAF to destruction.

Kesselring had suffered his first defeat, one in which absolute success would have been next to a miracle. By December, he was in doubt about the value of continuing these costly raids upon Britain. Then he learned of Germany's future plans for the East. Over the winter of 1940-41, Kesselring was made aware of the plans for Operation Barbarossa and learned of his role as the leading airman in this upcoming, earth shaking campaign, designed to annihilate Russia.

On June 13, 1941, he left the Channel coast to attend Hitler's final conference on Barbarossa. Officially however, he retained command in the West in order to keep alive the fiction that Germany had no plans other than the continuance of the war against England. Then, on June 22, 1941, the Germans struck Russia with a massive three prong assault.

Luftflotte II was once more assigned to von Bock's Army Group.

Von Bock was handed the starring role in this massive assault. His Army Group Centre was given the goal of capturing the Bolshevik capital, Moscow. Kesselring was quite content to be again working with von Bock, for there was true exemplary cooperation between them.

"All my commanders and I prided ourselves on anticipating the wishes of the Army and on carrying out any reasonable requests as quickly and as completely as we could."[5]

Kesselring's orders were to gain air superiority and, if possible, air supremacy and to support the Army, especially the Panzer Groups in their battle with the Russian Army.

With the opening of Barbarossa, never before or again would the German air crews have such an array of easy targets presented to them as on the first day. Within the time frame of a mere 24 hours, they had demolished the Soviet Air Force on almost every airfield within a 185 mile radius of the front. In two days, the Luftwaffe gained total air supremacy. Kesselring even felt confident enough to fly solo over the Russian zone, so completely was the destruction of the Soviet Air Force.

Kesselring found himself very active, flying to the front, scanning the battlefields, discussing situations with the local commanders, interviewing returning aircrews, giving praise and encouragement and, where necessary, sympathy or a reprimand. In the evening, he would return to his main headquarters for the daily conference at which the results of the day's activities were analyzed and the tasks for the next day mapped out.

Though not a part of the political-military wranglings of August and September, which saw the Germans change the shift of emphasis from the Centre to the South and then back again,

Kesselring could not help but comment that not going for Moscow after the capture of Smolensk in July was an error.

"The primary strategic objective had to be Moscow even if it involved a deliberate limitation of the objectives set for the Army Groups on the two wings."[6]

By October, the Germans again found Moscow to be their main objective. One-half of all Luftwaffe strength was allocated to Kesselring's command for this final drive on the Russian capital. After an optimistic start however, the weather closed in, making flying next to impossible. The Luftwaffe was strained to the limits. Besides flying combat missions, it was relegated to ferrying in supplies because of the deplorable state of the Russian road system, which effectively hampered moving supplies via truck.

The Luftwaffe suffered immensely as it too was feeling the pinch caused by dwindling supplies and worse yet, more aircraft were being lost than were being built. Kesselring felt that ultimate success would be denied the Germans. Soon however, Kesselring was to be lifted from the frozen Eastern Front to pursue his destiny in warmer climes.

In September, the German High Command had informed Kesselring, through Jeschonnek, the Luftwaffe Chief-of-Staff, that a stronger German presence was required in the Mediterranean. Kesselring was informed that he would therefore be reassigned to that area, not only as Luftwaffe Commander, but Theatre Commander-in-Chief as well.

Upon leaving Russia, Kesselring could look back with pride at the accomplishments of his air fleet. From June 22, until the time he relinquished command in late November, his air crews could boast of the destruction of 6,670 aircraft, 1,900 tanks, 1,950 guns, 26,000 motor vehicles and 2,800 trains.[7]

Before heading South, Kesselring was personally informed by Hitler that he must give priority to improving the unfavorable condition of the German supply line to North Africa. This problem soon became one of Kesselring's major concerns.

Arriving in Rome on November 28, 1941, he immediately sensed the difficulties in store for him, chief of which was the difficulty of waging coalition warfare. Kesselring however, soon proved himself the ideal man for the assignment. He was required to work with the Italians, of which the King and Mussolini were nominally his superiors, he had to work hard to control an ambitious General, Erwin Rommel, and he was compelled to satisfy a dictatorial leader, Adolf Hitler.

To please all would be a difficult, if not impossible task, and it would require a mastercraftsman in diplomacy to survive in this insane world of intrigue. His past experiences would come to serve him well. He had already demonstrated that he could handle people easily and he knew that the Italian position must be upheld sufficiently to satisfy their ego and to preserve their participation, but he also realized that the German cause must of course come first.

Kesselring surveyed the problem of the supply line and came to the conclusion that the British Island of Malta was the main nemesis. He was convinced that this strategic island would have to be physically occupied if it were to be neutralized. Thus, he set to work persuading Hitler and the OKW that an invasion of Malta was both feasible and imperative.

Flying to North Africa to survey the conditions first hand, he met the Italian leaders and the wily Rommel. The result of their discussions convinced him more than ever that the prime menace was Malta. No choice remained but to remove this threat.

In January, 1942, Malta was subjected to heavy bombing, placing the island's very survival in peril and thwarting the British efforts to attack the Axis convoys to North Africa. As a result, Rommel was granted a respite which allowed him the opportunity to replenish his supplies and refurbish his army. The devastating bombing assault continued throughout the first quarter of 1942, but meanwhile, Kesselring pressed Hitler, Goering, and the Italians to sanction the invasion of Malta.

In February, at a conference between Hitler and Mussolini, the project was approved in principle, but the actual plan was never really settled. They even went so far as to assign a code name to the project, Operation Hercules. Hitler however was apprehensive. The casualty list from the invasion of Crete* was still fresh in his mind and he seemed reluctant to condone a repeat performance. Likewise, the Italians appeared cool towards the entire concept.

By April 11, Kesselring was able to announce that Malta, as a naval base, no longer demanded consideration. Now was the time to strike. From his previous experience, Kesselring knew that air attacks alone could not bring about total victory unless they were immediately followed up by a land attack. Dunkirk and the Battle of Britain had proven that. But still the Italian and German Naval Staffs wavered. Kesselring states:

"That this did not happen was a grave mistake on the part of the German-Italian Command which came home to roost later."[8]

Rommel however, intervened to convince Hitler that Tobruk must first be taken. The German leader, thirsting for quick and inexpensive victories and thinking that Malta would prove too tough a nut to crack, was all too willing to let Rommel attack Tobruk before going for Malta. Kesselring disagreed and insisted that Malta should receive first consideration. The very fact that Rommel's supplies were built up to such a

*Crete was invaded in May, 1941. Though conquered, the heavy casualties incurred detracted from the victory.

point that he was ready for an offensive was proof that Malta, in German hands, would go a long way in assuring Axis domination of the Mediterranean. If Rommel could have known about the British code breaking abilities, perhaps he would have agreed to the elimination of Malta, for without this island, the British would be compelled to withdraw their naval forces to either end of the Mediterranean, their bases at Alexandria and Gibralter. In addition, air attacks against Axis convoys would be restricted to long range bombing. If they were unable to reach the convoys, knowing which routes the ships were following would be irrelevant. Unaware of this, and concentrating solely on ground operations, Rommel, and with him Hitler, agreed to attack the Gazala Line with the destination of Tobruk. After Tobruk, Malta could then be reconsidered.

For the support of Rommel's offensive against the British manning the positions in the Gazala Line, Kesselring assembled some 260 aircraft by May 26. It galled him to delay the assault on Malta, but he realized that the faster Rommel reached Tobruk, the quicker he would be able to order an assault against this island. Unfortunately, the British base at Malta was already

---

*Contrary to popular belief, Rommel, by this time, commanded an Italo-German formation designated Panzerarmee Afrika. Command of the Afrika Korps was left in the hands of a succession of subordinates, Cruewell amongst them.

showing signs of re-awakening.

During the Gazala battle, Kesselring flew over the battle zone, offering whatever assistance he could. General Westphal has said, "no other German Luftwaffe commander ever came up to Kesselring in his endeavors to help the Army".[9] When General Cruewell, commander of the Afrika Korps*, was captured after his plane was forced to land behind enemy lines, Kesselring, a Field Marshal, subordinated himself to Rommel, who held the inferior rank of Colonel General, and assumed Cruewell's command until a substitute was found.

Tobruk fell on June 21, and with its fall, Kesselring once more pushed for the initiation of Hercules. But Rommel had other ideas. Hercules was vetoed and Hitler allowed Rommel to proceed to Cairo. Kesselring could only caution of the dire results should Malta be left unmolested.

Over the summer of 1942, Kesselring saw disaster looming near. With Malta rapidly regaining its former potency, he realized that everything now depended on Rommel's striking into the British at the El Alamein line as quickly as possible, before the latter had the opportunity to grow stronger. Thwarted in his efforts to have Malta attacked, Kesselring felt that the only avenue was to urge Rommel into an offensive to break the Alamein line and push on to Cairo and the Suez Canal.

The result was the ill-fated Battle of Alam el Halfa of August 30, 1942. Minefields, British air activity and of course the British pre-knowledge through Ultra, coupled with the growing striking power of Malta which was again wreaking havoc with Axis convoys, contributed to a major Axis defeat at the hands of General Bernard L. Montgomery. With this defeat, Kesselring realized that the fate of the North African campaign was sealed. Henceforward, his major preoccupation was the consolidation of the Axis position in order to keep the Allies from influencing the European Theatre for as long as possible.

In October, Kesselring assumed responsibility for the defense of all Axis occupied coastal areas in the Mediterranean. He thus became the only German officer to control all three services in joint command. Shortly thereafter, on October 23, 1942, the British Eighth Army, under the command of General Bernard Montgomery, struck from the El Alamein Line. Rommel happened to be away in Germany on sick leave and in his place was General George Stumme who, on the first day of battle, suffered a fatal heart attack.

Rommel was immediately recalled to North Africa, but the situation was critical for the Axis forces. The Desert Fox, seeing the desperate plight of his forces, ordered a withdrawal on November 3, only to have this order countermanded by Hitler, who refused to sanction any retreat. Kesselring however, realized the desperate plight and radioed the Fuhrer a brief summary of the situation, highlighting the consequences that would unquestionably follow if Rommel were not allowed to retreat. He added a request that Rommel be granted a free hand. Hitler promptly complied. Rommel's Army thus escaped, thanks to the skill of its commander, the lack of aggression on Montgomery's part, and of course, the tactfulness of Kesselring.

Besides worrying about Rommel's forces, Kesselring also had to consider the possibility of an Allied landing in Northwest Africa. The possibility became a reality on November 8, when a combined Anglo-American Army landed at three different areas along the Northwest coast of Africa. With Montgomery advancing from the East and the Allied landing in the West, a giant pincer was about to close on Rommel.

On November 9, Hitler authorized Kesselring to do whatever he thought necessary to control the situation. The latter felt that the Axis should immediately occupy French Tunisia, which up till that time, Hitler disallowed because of his previous agreements with the Vichy government. When the French in North Africa cast their lot with the Allies however, Hitler declared these agreements null and void and sanctioned whatever action Kesselring deemed necessary.

On November 15, General Walter Nehring, late of the Afrika Korps, arrived to take command in Tunisia. Kesselring realized the need for a Panzer Army Headquarters in Tunisia and his request was quickly granted. At the beginning of December, General Jurgen von Arnim took command of the newly created Fifth Panzer Army.

In the meantime, Rommel was bombarding

Kesselring with requests for supplies which the latter was unable to fill. Not only had Malta become the same great menace it was in 1941, but supplies were now urgently required in large quantities for Tunisia. This country was to be turned into a base from which the Axis hoped to dispose of the threat from both the East and West.

Kesselring was determined to build up a bridgehead in Tunisia before the Allies drove there in strength. Fortunately for him, the Allies were busy consolidating their position in Morocco and Algeria and thus, did not drive directly for Tunisia. Kesselring knew that:

"Our strategic objective must be to keep the two armies apart and to attack and defeat them, one after the other from an interior line."[10]

With this in mind, the Axis conceived the offensive that led to the American baptism of fire at Kasserine Pass. Since Eisenhower's forces were ahead of Montgomery's, it was planned to attack the former first, before turning against the latter.

Though seriously disrupting the Americans at Kasserine, all Axis attacks failed to achieve the anticipated level of success. Jealousy over command perogatives between Rommel and von Arnim plus the shaky Italian resolve, contributed to Kesselring's problems.

During the few months remaining to the Axis

forces in Tunisia, Kesselring commuted regularly between that country, Rome and Berlin, trying to drum up promises of support from Hitler and his entourage; promises which were rarely honored. He constantly tried to steady the shaky resolve of the Italians and was endlessly pleading for supplies for the formations in Tunisia.

Kesselring not only realized the difficulties of holding out in Tunisia, but also recognized that the longer he could hold out, the longer the Allies would be delayed from moving into Southern Europe, their next obvious objective.

The Allied offensive that sealed the fate of the Axis forces in North Africa was launched on March 20, 1943 with an assault on the Mareth Line by the British Eighth Army. By March 27, this line had to be abandoned and the end of the Tunisian campaign was clearly in sight.

With the end obviously near, Kesselring wished to comb out essential personnel, but Hitler refused because he feared that this move would adversely affect morale. Consequently, all Kesselring was able to accomplish was the evacuation of only a few essential military personalities, along with all flying formations and surface ships.

Squeezed into a corner with the sea to their backs, the Axis forces fought until no hope remained. On May 13, 1943, von Arnim surrendered his command with over 250,000 troops, which were sent off to POW Camps.

With the fall of North Africa, an assault into

Southern Europe seemed inevitable. From January, 1943, Kesselring attempted to anticipate the possible moves of the Allies in the Mediterranean. Sicily of course, was one of the possible targets. However, there were other areas to which high priority was given; Corsica, Sardinia and the Balkans. Though favoring the former as the next Allied move, the deceptive operations conducted by the Allies, foremost being "Operation Mincemeat"*, threw the Axis off the track as to the exact Allied intention.

The question was finally answered on July 10, 1943, when two Allied armies under Patton and Montgomery stormed ashore at Sicily.

The eve of the Allied invasion of Sicily found twelve Italian and two mobile German divisions on that island, plus three more divisions on the Italian mainland and two more en route.

Kesselring took an extremely active part in the Sicilian defense, going so far as to employing direct German channels of communication with German formations and ordering attacks without waiting for instructions or obtaining the approval of the Italians.

On July 12, after ordering the 1st Parachute Division to be flown over to the island, Kesselring himself flew into Sicily. Accompanied by the very capable General von Senger, he visited the front line positions and personally witnessed the total breakdown of the Italian divisions and

*Deceptive plan designed to deceive the Germans as to where the Allies would land.

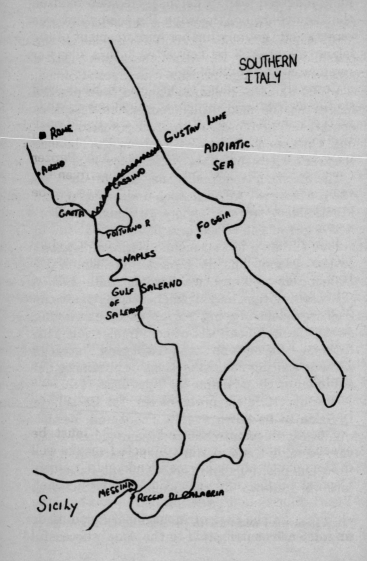

SOUTHERN
ITALY

ROME

Anzio

Gaeta

Cassino

Volturno R

Naples

Gulf
of
Salerno

Salerno

Gustav Line

ADRIATIC
SEA

Foggia

Messina

Reggio Di Calabria

Sicily

the tactical chaos resulting from their disregard for the agreed plan of defense. He soon realized that any chance of throwing the enemy out was remote and that any further reinforcement of the island might well be converted into a disaster reminiscent of Tunisia.

Correctly concluding that Western Sicily held no tactical value, he ordered it abandoned, while at the same time constructing a defensive position around Mt. Etna, which area was to be held until the island was evacuated. The XIV Panzer Corps commander, General Hube, was given the assignment to dig in. Yes, Sicily was to be evacuated, but Hube's job as to delay this move as long as possible.

Kesselring was now issuing direct orders, completely by-passing the Italian command structure. Truly, the Italian position had become quite doubtful. Then came a severe blow; Mussolini fell from power. The controversy that developed over this situation was fated to embroil Kesselring in a deep controversy with Rommel, and, even worse, cost Kesselring the confidence of Hitler. Before analyzing this however, we must first examine the end of the Sicilian campaign.

Though it was obvious that Sicily must be evacuated, the way it was conducted speaks well of the quality of the German leadership, namely General Hube and the Commander-in-Chief, Field Marshal Kesselring. Of course, the slowness on the part of Montgomery also made an immense contribution to the Axis' successful evacuation of Sicily.

"The enemy failure to exploit the last chance
of hindering the German forces crossing the
Straits of Messina, by continuous and
strongly coordinated attacks from the sea and
the air, was almost a greater boon to the German command than their failure immediately
to push their pursuit across the straits on 17
August."[11]

Kesselring therefore was able to evacuate the
German forces virtually intact, a feat of great
magnitude, since the Allies had command of the
air and the sea. Now however, what was he to do
next.

Mussolini was gone and a doubtful government under Marshal Badoglio was in his place.
Though Badoglio was noisily making promises
of continuing the alliance, the German High
Command had many reservations. Kesselring's
optimism cost him Hitler's trust and he was
branded an Italophile because of his trust of the
Italians. Rommel was attempting to convince
Hitler that the best strategy for the Germans
was to evacuate southern Italy, stating in his
conclusion, that it would be suicidal to remain in
the south, for the Allies, possessing superior
naval forces, would find it easy to make an amphibious landing behind any German defense,
resulting in an encirclement and subsequent
destruction of the defenders.

Kesselring trusted the Italians, and wished to

maintain an open dialogue with Badoglio. Relations between Hitler and Kesselring became so bad that, on August 23, at three in the morning, Hitler told Kesselring, in Goering's presence, that he had received infallible proof of Italy's treachery. He begged Kesselring to stop being a dupe of the Italians and begin to prepare to deal with their treachery.

Refusing to trust the Italians, Hitler moved Rommel's Army Group B into northern Italy. He also ordered German troops flown into Rome from France, in order to reinforce the German Garrison there. Meanwhile, German troops were evacuating Sicily. In addition, troops were also being withdrawn from Sardinia and Corsica. Once these withdrawals were complete, and all German troops safely on the mainland, Rommel would take complete command of all German forces. Kesselring seemed to have reached the nadir of his career.

However, he kept an avenue of communication open between himself and Badoglio in order to hold the Axis together. Gradually, his policy was becoming accepted by some Germans, who felt that perhaps the alliance could be kept together. Call it naivete, but Kesselring clung to the hope that he would be able to work with the new Italian Government. Little did he realize however, that at that very time, during August and early September, Italian peace envoys were seeking ways of reaching a settlement with the Allies.

Kesselring was not completely blind though.

The Germans had a plan called 'Plan Axis', which, in the event of an Italian surrender, they would put into effect. In his autobiography he states:

"My chief endeavour was to keep a firm leash on the Italian troops and so on the Italian command."[12]

If Italy surrendered, Kesselring would evacuate endangered fronts, essential stores were, as far as possible, to be hidden, and a bargain was to be made with the Italian commanders in order to help the Germans escape. All serviceable aircraft and anti-aircraft guns were to be captured and the Italian Navy was to be prevented from putting out to sea. Furthermore, the Germans were to occupy all important military signal stations and lastly, the King and Badoglio were to be taken prisoner.

This period produced a terrible strain on Kesselring's nerves. Hitler's harsh statements and lack of trust, together with the burden of military work and the increasing tempo of Allied air attacks on Italy, not to mention the possibility of Italian doubledealing, to a man such as Kesselring proved a heavy burden. One that required every bit of his ability to handle.

What would the Allies do after Sicily? On September 3, four years since the British declaration of war, the Allies played their first card with the invasion of southern Italy, across the Straits of Messina, by Montgomery's Eighth

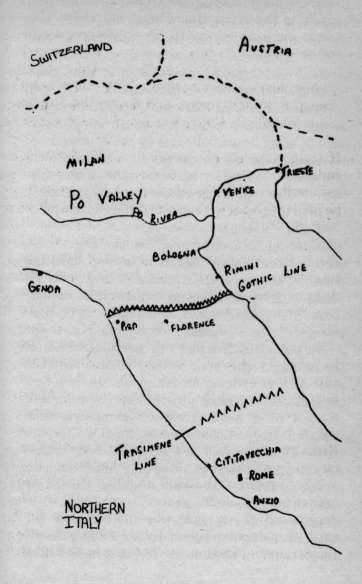

Army. Typically, Montgomery's advance was slow and the Germans felt secure that they would not have to unduly concern themselves with that advance. But, when they spotted the Allied Fleet steaming north, it filled them with much foreboding.

Where could that fleet be heading? North or south of Rome? North or south of Naples? Should a landing take place in the Naples area, Kesselring saw no necessity for evacuating central Italy. However, he was quite distraught with Hitler's attitude of writing off the eight German divisions in the south of Italy. Why not send more instead?

Kesselring attempted to explain the importance of containing the Allies as far south as possible. He was convinced that to evacuate the whole of Italy and defend the Reich from positions in the Alps would be against the best interests of the Germans, for it would give the Allies unlimited freedom of movement either in the direction of France or the Balkans. It would also mean sacrificing an indispensable deep battle zone, thus opening up southern Germany and Austria to a devastating air campaign from northern Italy. Consequently, he felt that the battle for Italy was not only justified, it was mandatory. It seemed however, that Rommel's ideas had infected the Fuhrer and so Kesselring was left to his own devices.

On September 8, 1943, yet another blow fell. Word of the Italian surrender struck him deeply but he could, in all honesty, feel that he had done all that was humanly possible to save the Axis alliance.

Kesselring found out about the surrender in a rather strange way. Bombs fell upon his headquarters in Frascati, temporarily causing the evacuation of his offices. Subsequently, he received word from Jodl of the OKW informing him that a radio message had been received announcing the surrender of Italy. Jodl wished to know if it was indeed true. Kesselring notified the Italian government and was informed that the message was a deliberate Allied hoax and that Italy had every intention of honoring the alliance and continuing the war. He then ordered the Italians to issue an official denial, but it was never made. Again Jodl called him to tell him that the Fuhrer General Headquarters had received a wireless message from Badoglio, admitting to the surrender. Thus, the situation was now rather unclear for Kesselring.

Plan Axis was immediately activated and he concentrated on securing Rome and its environs. At Fuhrer Headquarters, Kesselring's command was immediately written off as lost. Kesselring knew he must act, and act fast. He sent a message to the Tenth Army Commander.

"Italian troops will be asked to continue the fight on our side by appeals to their honor. Those who refuse are to be ruthlessly disarmed. No mercy must be shown to traitors. Long live the Fuhrer."[13]

Luckily for the Germans, the Italians were more shaken than they. The Germans held the initiative and, by bluff and subterfuge, were able to obtain the surrender of many troops along with their weapons, equipment and supplies. Kesselring's command lucked out again when the King and Badoglio escaped from Rome and were inescapable of asserting any influence on the conduct of events.

In Rome, there was still a sizable Italian force awaiting reinforcement from an expected Allied airborne attack. In fact, a United States airborne division was standing by, prepared to disembark for Rome. But, at the last minute, the operation was cancelled due to the risk involved.

When, on September 9, with the Allied landing at Salerno, Kesselring rested easier, secure in the knowledge that Rome was not the next target. Westphal, Kesselring's Chief-of-Staff, was convinced that if persuasion were applied, the Italians might surrender the city. By evening of the 9th, the Italians and Germans had discussed a possible tentative agreement whereby Rome was to be declared an open city. This would allow the Germans to maintain their embassy and main communications center. The Italian troops, however, were required to lay down their arms, but they would be allowed to work for the Germans and would still be in charge of maintaining order. To convince them of the folly of resistance, Kesselring applied pressure on the Italians, warning them that should they not accept the stated terms, he would order the demolition of the aqueducts and the bombardment of Rome.

Throughout the night the Italians deliberated. By the 10th, with the realization that Salerno was the only main Allied effort and aware that the Italian people and soldiers had no heart for renewed hostilities, he demanded total capitulation. He personally entered the conference room and insisted that the Italian delegates sign the agreement and deliver it to him by 4 P.M. If not, Rome would be bombed. Compliance was swift and Kesselring had earned a victory with the absolute minimum of force. He had saved the Germans from what might have been a first rate disaster.

The choice of Salerno by the Allies was seen by Kesselring as a blessing. Hearing of the landing, he knew that it would be necessary that the two German divisions in Calabria be hastened northward, but at the same time, Montgomery's progress must be delayed. Here the Germans found themselves aided by the mountainous terrain.

Meanwhile, the Hermann Goering Division was ordered to Salerno and Luftflotte II sent against the Allied invasion fleet. Without aid from Hitler and Rommel, Kesselring was forced to deal with the beachhead with those few forces available. By the end of the first day, he was satisfied with the situation at Salerno.

"The fighting on the beaches of Salerno despite the Allies' overwhelming air superiority, tremendous naval gunfire and our numerical weakness, went better than I had dared hope."[14]

Eventually, however, without the hope of reinforcements from Rommel's Army Group in the North, the overwhelming forces assembled by the Allies would cause Kesselring to relinquish Salerno, but not before his forces almost accomplished the elimination of the American beachhead under the command of General Mark Clark. Thanks to Montgomery's slow advance, the U.S. Fifth Army was almost thrown back into the sea, but they held on by a very narrow thread. Kesselring realized however, that superior Allied air and naval power would eventually tell and, coupled with the inevitable assistance from Montgomery, Salerno would have to be abandoned.

Kesselring's withdrawal was not to the north of Italy however. Both Rommel and Hitler advocated this move but their advice fell on deaf ears. Kesselring was determined to keep the Allies confined as far south as possible, with or without support.

By September 10, his strategy was already laid down.

"I had already drawn on the map our successive defense positions in the event of a retirement from southern Italy."[15]

On September 12, Mussolini was freed from

captivity by a daring raid conducted by the notorious SS Commando, Otto Skorzeny. The former dictator was immediately restored as the leader of Italy. However, he was relegated to being what he had actually been for some time, a mere puppet of the Germans.

Though forced to relinquish ground, Kesselring was optimistic over the possibility of going over to the defensive south of Rome, using the terrain as an ally. By using the spiny backbone of Italy, he deemed it possible that, from the east coast to the west, he would be able to establish impenetrable defensive lines. It would be left to General von Vietinghoff's Tenth Army to gain the time Kesselring desperately needed to build his fortifications around the Cassino area where the defensive line would stop the Allies in their tracks. This line was designated the Gustav Line.

Though still favoring the retirement to a position well north of Rome, gradually Hitler's advisors, except those favoring Rommel, began to comprehend the logic of Kesselring's policy of gradual withdrawal with a pinning down of the Allied Armies on successive lines of defense. As Kesselring's policies seemed to warrant merit and were obviously achieving a level of success, Hitler began to waver and lean more towards the former's point of view.

What had the Germans gained from Kesselring's quick defensive actions at Salerno?

"They had denied the Allies quick access to

Naples. They had inflicted severe losses on the Allied troops. Avoiding the dangers implicit in the simultaneous occurrences of the Italian surrender announcement and the Allied invasion, they had extricated their forces from southern Italy. By preventing the Allies from breaking out of the beachhead, a feat the Germans accomplished despite shortages of fuel and lengthy lines of communication, they had prohibited the Allies from fully exploiting the Italian surrender."[16]

General Alexander admitted that the Germans may claim, with some justification, to have won, if not a victory, then at least an important success over the Allies. The real test, however, was yet to come.

At successive meetings, Kesselring described to Hitler the advantages of his strategy, particularly emphasizing that fewer troops would be needed because of the nature of the Italian terrain which benefited the defenders. Finally, after many debates, Hitler swung around to Kesselring's side and decided that Rommel would remain in the north, but Kesselring was to stay on in the south where he was to prove the soundness of his strategy. Hitler further ordered two divisions transferred from Rommel's command to Kesselring's.

Kesselring was now fighting not just for the defense of Italy, but for his reputation as well. Bringing pressure to bear upon his subordinates, he moved from place to place filling his men with a driving determination to utilize every means to foil the Allied advance.

Upon leaving Salerno, the Germans retreated to the first of the delaying lines, the Volturno River. Von Vietinghoff was giving Kesselring the time he needed to construct the Gustav Line. The Tenth Army Commander was told that he must hold the Allies at the Volturno until at least October 15. He carried out this order superbly and held the position till October 16, when he retreated to the next line, the Bernhardt Line (Reinhardt) which the Allies called the Winter Line. Kesselring held high hopes that this position would also hold.

From east to west the Allies assaulted the German position, placing Kesselring in the awkward position of fighting a defensive battle while constructing defenses. He also lived in constant fear that the Allies might assault his rear. Yet he pulled it off despite Allied naval and aerial supremacy.

On October 25, Hitler was sufficiently impressed with the performance of Kesselring. He therefore decided to send Rommel elsewhere, giving Kesselring overall command in Italy. On November 3, Rommel was dispatched to France and Kesselring assumed command of Army Group C, incorporating all German forces in the theatre on November 21. Kesselring thus held a joint position, Commander-in-Chief of Army Group C and Commander-in-Chief South West. Even though Mussolini was the so-called ruler,de facto, Kesselring was actual ruler, a true consul.

The Field Marshal was a busy man. One of his staff officers has written.

"About 8 o'clock in the morning the Field Marshal received the daily reports and worked in general until midnight with a short break at lunch time. On at least 3 days a week, and sometimes more, the Field Marshal went to visit units at the front."[17]

Action at the front fully absorbed the Commander-in-Chief. He was determined to maintain the front at bearable cost in a campaign which was attritional, and to make the cost of every inch of Italian soil prohibitive for the Allies. Luckily for Kesselring, the Allies found themselves handicapped by limitation of resources. Their major reason for fighting in Italy was to tie down German forces in order to make the upcoming cross channel invasion from England to France a success. With that operation holding the priority for resources, the Allied Armies were forced to fight with relatively limited men and resources.

Italian warfare was positional warfare and Kesselring was a master at this type of combat, fighting in terrain that catered to his talents. Such terrain features as Monte Camino, Monte La Defensa, Monte Maggiore, and Monte Lungo will long be remembered by both German and Allied forces for the bloody battles of that Fall of 1943. The German defense of San Pietro historically represents one of the most stubborn defenses of the entire Italian campaign. Nature provided the Germans generously, but Kesselring improved on what nature provided.

By the middle of January, the scene had been set for what was to be the greatest test yet in Italy, the Allied attack on the vaunted Gustav Line. The United States Official History states:

"The line was rooted in the high ground backing the Gargliano and Rapido Rivers. In the hills behind the Gargliano in the Saint Ambrogio area, on the steep and barren slopes of Monte Cassino, and among the jumbled mountain peaks near the source of the Rapido, the Germans had blasted and dug weapons pits, built concrete bunkers and steel-turreted machine gun emplacements, strung bands of barbed wire and planted mine fields—making lavish use of the box mine, which was difficult to detect because it had almost no metallic parts to block the few natural avenues of advance. They had sited mortars on reverse slopes and placed automatic weapons to cover the forward slopes. In the town of Cassino they had strengthened the walls of the stone buildings with sandbags to protect weapons crews"[18]

On January 17, the British X Corps of Fifth Army launched an assault across the lower reaches of the Gargliano River. It achieved surprise and a deeper penetration than the German commander felt acceptable. Von Vietinghoff called Kesselring for reserves. The latter, being assured by Admiral Canaris, head of German intelligence, that the Allies would not conduct an amphibious assault in the Rome area, sent two divisions to the Gustav Line. Though the British had dented the line, he felt it was not the main Allied effort. He was convinced that the main direction was pointed up the Liri Valley, the gateway to Rome, a direction in which the British were not pointing.

Rather, an American thrust across the Rapido River to the south of Cassino seemed logical. Here, Kesselring was sure, was the endangered area.

On January 20, the American 36th Division attacked across the Rapido and were stopped with terrible losses for the famous Texas Division. The presence of the two reserve divisions which hindered the British X Corps from aiding the Americans dashed Mark Clark's dreams of breaking the Gustav Line, those hopes vanishing in that stream of blood.

Since November, the Allies had been considering the possibility of an amphibious landing behind the German Lines. Through political wrangling and string pulling, the Allies formulated a plan to land at Anzio, thirty miles south of Rome. It was considered that this would place the Allies in an excellent position to circumvent the Gustav Line and allow them to attack the Germans from the rear.

When the Allies landed at Anzio on January 22, 1944, it proved a momentary embarassment for Kesselring. His initial response was one of anger. However, he immediately grasped the situation. Von Vietinghoff was of the opinion that the Gustav Line should be evacuated, but Kesselring responded in the negative. He elected instead, to play the gambler. Thanks to the hesitancy of the American VII Corps' commander, General Lucas, a respite was gained. The latter felt that building up the beachhead was his primary objective prior to advancing to the Alban Hills where he was to sever the access routes of the German Tenth Army. Although complete surprise was achieved at Anzio, and Rome was ripe for the picking, Lucas threw away his advantage and elected to sit still on the beach. Kesselring was thus able to exploit the situation by bringing together a higgledy-piggledy jumble of different units under the command of General Eberhard von Mackensen, late of the Russian front. This force was designated Fourteenth Army.

Von Mackensen was given two tasks; to strengthen the defense ring around the beachhead and to initiate measures to narrow and remove it. By the time Lucas was ready to move, the Fourteenth Army was in place and the Allies were halted in their tracks, suffering severe losses. Kesselring now found two fronts to defend, the Gustav Line and the Anzio area. He had however, achieved a great success. "Experience and luck had been his salvation."[19]

With the Anzio offensive bogged down, the Allies struck once more at the Gustav Line. The fighting around Cassino and its historic Benedictine Monastery reached brutal proportions. Between February 15-19, the Allies, for the second time, attempted to breach the Gustav Line. This time, the 4th Indian Division of North African fame and the New Zealand Corps attempted to capture Cassino and the monastery by direct assault. The failure of this attempt caused General Freyberg, the New Zealand commander, to decide that the monestery was being used by the Germans and he called for its destruction. In defense of this Kesselring has stated:

"Once and for all I wish to establish the fact that the monastery was not occupied as part of the line."[20]

That the Allies destroyed the monastery even after German assurances that they were not occupying it, was a sure sign to the German protoganists that the Allies were barbarians. Once the monastery was bombed to destruction by the Allied Air Forces, the Germans felt no obligation towards this holy area and occupied the rubble, which gave them a superior concrete fortress.

Meanwhile, at Anzio, the struggle was in full progress. The American attack having failed, von Mackensen now attempted to eliminate the beachhead. Though some temporary success was initially registered, the overall offensive did not accomplish its objective and a stalemate settled over the front. Though not successful, the Germans could take pride in the fact that they had foiled the primary purpose of the Anzio landing. It now became a matter of who was pinning down whom. Kesselring never let up on the air and artillery assaults, making the Anzio beachhead one vast constant battlefield. No place was haven and the Allies were forced to move underground for safety.

In March, another attempt by the Allies to take Cassino was again repulsed. After this offensive, a lull developed over the battlefield with each side licking its wounds and taking stock of its resources. Kesselring realized that it was mandatory for the Germans to build up large reserves if they were to withstand the inevitable offensive. It was apparant to him that the Allies would try to link up the southern front with the Anzio beachhead. He also anticipated the danger of yet another Allied landing north of Rome.

In March, an incident occurred that was to have a long range effect on Kesselring at his post-war trial in 1947. Communist partisans placed a bomb which, when exploded, killed 32 German SS policemen and 8 Italian citizens. Hitler subsequently ordered the execution of 10 Italians for every German killed. Though legally not to blame for the shooting of the Italians in the Ardealine Caves, Kesselring was given the death sentence in 1947. One of the charges registered against him was this incident. It is true that Kesselring despised partisans, most professional soldiers do. His attitude went back to 1919 when he witnessed the terror of the Communist partisans in Germany. In his memoirs, he documentated his hatred of this type of warfare. This hatred came to haunt him during the postwar trials.

On May 11, 1944, there seemed little danger of an Allied offensive striking immediately. Faulty German intelligence caused Kesselring to send three divisions north to Leghorn to protect against a potential amphibious landing. In addition, five divisions were sent to the Fourteenth Army at Anzio and two others were sent into reserve, leaving only nine divisions at the Gustav Line opposing the fifteen of the Allies.

Then operation Diadem struck with a fury onto the German positions. The fighting was fierce and costly, with the Germans bravely defending their positions. In the long run, however, they proved too weak against the superior Allied forces. By May 19, it was obvious that the Tenth Army required immediate reinforcement if the Gustav Line were to hold, so Kesselring transferred the 29th Panzer Grenadiers from the Fourteenth Army. Von Mackensen opposed the transfer and Kesselring personally had to convince him of the importance of the transfer. The move, however, was too late and the 29th Panzer Grenadiers were forced to fight from unprepared positions with disastrous results.

The Germans were forced to fall back from the Gustav Line to the next line of prepared defenses, the Senger Line, formerly known as the Hitler Line. Again the Germans employed the tactics for which they had become famous and earned valuable time by delaying the Allies.

Then, on May 22, the Anzio forces, under a new commander, General Lucian Truscott, broke loose from their shackles. The following day, the Canadians in the Eighth Army cracked the Senger Line and poured up the Liri Valley with the French keeping pace on their left and the Americans along the coast seeking to link up with the Anzio forces.

With the breakout at Anzio, Kesselring's forces were facing disaster. Thanks to the ambitions of Mark Clark, however, the Germans were given a respite and avoided complete destruction.

General Alexander ordered Clark to send VI Corps to Valmontone which, if taken, would sever the escape route of the German Tenth Army. Instead, Clark sought immortality and decided to go straight for Rome. Altering Alexander's orders to suit his own purpose, he sent a token force to Valmontone and redirected the bulk of VI Corps towards Rome. Clark however, found his way temporarily barred by von Mackensen who correctly guessed the American's desires. This allowed von Vietinghoff time to fall back to the next delaying position, the Caesar Line.

The Caesar Line was not as strong as the Gustav Line, but it was the last defensive position before Rome. At this point, von Mackensen and Kesselring differed over enemy intentions. The former felt he knew the enemy's intention so he deployed his main strength in the hills southwest of Rome. This resulted in a wide gap between the Tenth and Fourteenth Armies. Kesselring pressured von Mackensen to fill that gap to no avail. The Fourteenth Army commander was convinced that he knew better. To his credit, von Mackensen did have Clark figured correctly but the overwhelming effect of the Allied attack was just too much for the Germans to withstand and as a result, Rome was entered on June 4. Clark had his moment of glory.

It is to Kesselring's lasting credit and his love for Rome that he declared it an open city, ordering that it was not to be defended. Furthermore, thanks to both Clark's ambitions and Kesselring's skill, most of the Tenth Army was able to slip unmolested east of Rome and the German retreat never once resembled a rout. However, the slowness of the Allied pursuit north of Rome definitely eased the situation for Kesselring.

As in 1943, Kesselring planned to delay the Allies in defensive positions, giving ground gradually in order to gain time for the construction of a more permanent defensive position in the northern Appenines.

For most of June, Kesselring was helping his commanders out of successive difficulties and giving ground without Hitler's permission. Whenever the Fuhrer indicated his displeasure, Kesselring would fly personally to present his case to the Fuhrer. Boldly he asked Hitler for a free hand.

"The point is not whether my Armies are

fighting or running away. I can assure you that they will fight and die if I ask it of them. We are talking about something entirely different, a question much more vital, whether after Stalingrad and Tunis you can afford the loss of yet two more armies. I beg to doubt it—the more so as if I change my plans to meet with your ideas, sooner or later the way into Germany will be opened to the Allies. On the other hand, I guarantee—unless my hands are tied—to delay the Allied advance appreciably, to halt it at latest in the Appenines, and by to create conditions for the prosecution of the war in 1944 which can be dovetailed into your general strategic scheme."[21]

Thus he guaranteed Hitler that the Allied advance would be halted, and he won his point.

"To no other commander, not even to favourites such as Goring, Guderian, or Rommel, did Hitler make such concessions at this stage of the war and, to all intents and purposes, keep his word thereafter."[22]

By mobile tactics, the Germans gradually stiffened the front. Kesselring's intention was to present a longer resistance on narrow and more favourably located fronts and abandon the less favourable sectors. Delaying the Allies was the key.

On July 20, the plot against Hitler failed. Kesselring, a man who took his oath seriously, immediately sought to demonstrate that he was unaware of the conspiracy and verbally reaffirmed his loyalty to the German dictator.

Thanks to political and military decisions within the Allied camp, troops were withdrawn from the fighting front in order to prepare for the invasion of southern France. With the departure of these troops, particularly the crack French Expeditionary Corps and the United States 3, 45, and 36 Divisions, the Allied forces found themselves greatly weakened making it easier for Kesselring to apply his delaying tactics.

The Allied pursuit continued however, and by August, the Germans had moved into their positions in the Appenines, designated the Gothic Line.^ There, Kesselring, conducted many fierce battles all along the line, especially on the Adriatic front where the British attempted to circumvent the mountains by attacking towards Rimini. Some local British success was registered but then, with the onset of Autumn rains, the Allied attack petered out and ground to a halt.

Bologna and the Po River vally were the eventual Allied objectives and, once these goals were reached, the mountains would then be behind them and the rich, flat, Po Valley would be exposed to them. It was therefore crucial to stop the Allies from breaking the Gothic Line fortifications in the northern Appenines.

Hitler also recognized the importance of stopping the Allies. The Po Valley, with its impor-

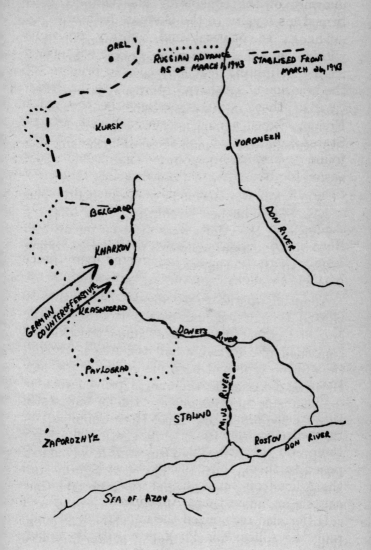

ORL

RUSSIAN ADVANCE
AS OF MARCH 11, 1943

STABLISED FRONT
MARCH 26, 1943

KURSK

VORONEZH

DON RIVER

BELGOROD

KHARKOV

GERMAN COUNTEROFFENSIVE

KRASNOGRAD

DONETS RIVER

PAVLOGRAD

MIUS RIVER

STALINO

ZAPOROZHYE

ROSTON

DON RIVER

SEA OF AZOV

tant industries were too important to be lost for the Reich. In addition, the shock effect loss of this area would have on the German people was immeasurable and required consideration. Kesselring still felt as he did a year before, the Allies must be halted as far south as possible.

The fighting during that Fall of 1944 was filled with heavy casualties on both sides. Thanks, however, to the deteriorating weather, Kesselring was allowed a small sense of optimism. The Allies had suffered heavily.

> "For while the Germans were down fifty percent of established strength in their infantry divisions, the Allies were little better off and deprived of reinforcements which were being sent to other theatres."[23]

Adapting to the Allied drives, he constantly shifted boundaries and moved troops. By the end of October, the weather and attrition had combined to effectively halt the Allies. Though the Gothic Line had been pierced in spots, new German defenses further north proved just as impenetrable and Bologna and the Po Valley still seemed distant to the Allied High Command.

On October 23, 1944, while visiting the front during a rain storm, Kesselring was involved in a violent collision with the barrel of a large gun emerging from a side turning. He suffered a fractured skull, his face was severely lacerated, and he lay unconscious for 12 hours. Though he eventually recovered, he was out of action for three months. While recuperating, his position was filled by General von Vietinghoff who proceeded in the manner of Kesselring.

By the middle of January, he was back in Italy. Upon returning he commented,

"I found that the Allies, as expected had made constant attrition thrusts against our lines, and though success had been only local, and not in any way decisive, they had blunted the mettle of our troops."[24]

Nevertheless, he found troop morale good and the determination to hold on just as strong as ever.

With the Winter snow effectively hindering offensive action, Kesselring realized that the Allies would attack as soon as Spring came. Then, suddenly, on March 8, 1945, he was summoned by Hitler who appointed him Commander-in-Chief of the Western Front, effective March 10. Thus, after almost three and one-half years in the Mediterranean, Kesselring found himself called to another theatre.

Had the Italian campaign been worth it? Rommel, as we have already seen, felt that once Italy surrendered, evacuation to the Alps was the only viable alternative. Kesselring failed to share that conviction, for he felt that the evacuation of the whole of Italy would force the Germans to defend the Reich from Alpine positions which would have allowed the Allies too much freedom either to move into southern France or the Balkans. It would also have opened the area of southern Germany and Austria to a devastating air campaign launched from northern Italy. Kesselring promised Hitler that he would hold Italy until 1945 and, through his determination and skill, kept that promise.

The battle for Italy was one conducted with a high degree of proficiency and speaks highly for the skill of the man who managed to keep the Allies from Rome for nine months, who overcame the obstacle presented by the Italian surrender, an amphibious attack in his rear, and costly partisan attacks. Though eventually forced to retreat, it was always conducted with a high level of proficiency resulting in heavy losses registered on the side of the enemy. Remember, he accomplished all of this with the enemy holding domination of the sea and air and with his adversaries possessing the ability to read his secret messages via Ultra.

As far as the final outcome of the war, it mattered little if Italy were held, for ultimate victory can be traced to other theatres. Thus, the contribution to victory by Kesselring's Italian campaign was nugatory. However, by the fact that he achieved his major purposes and did manage to keep the Allies at bay for so long, demonstrated what a commander could do with the minimal interference from Hitler. If the Italian campaign were held up as an example of a military mastermind at work, then for the German war effort, the Italian campaign was well worth the effort. Kesselring's professional ability stands as a shining example of the quality of German military leadership. The very fact that Hitler turned to this genius in March of 1945, to become Commander-in-Chief West, speaks highly of the esteem in which he was held in the eyes of the German leader.

With the fall of Remagen and the capture of the Ludendorff Bridge spanning the Rhine in that resort town, Hitler felt the need for a change in command in the west. For the third and final time in the war, Field Marshall Gerd von Rundstedt was sent into retirement and Kesselring was directed to that front as his successor. He was given, as his major objective, the buying of time for Germany so that new fighters and other novel weapons could be employed that would turn the tide in Germany's favor. "My mission was clear, hang on." This was a role in which he excelled.

Kesselring spent his first few days going from one command post to another, examining the front first hand and, by the night of March 13, was able to form a superficial personal impression of the situation. In a word, it was obvious the Allies were superior both in numbers and material, and their Air Force dominated the battle zone. Kesselring, however, had his objective, to hang on, for the new weapons were on the way and time was required to reinforce the east in order to stop the advance of the dreaded Bolsheviks.

On March 15, Kesselring again discussed the situation with Hitler. Needless to say, he was handed a next to impossible task. Like a house of cards, the collapse was inevitable. Filling the gaps caused by Allied breakthroughs became selfdefeating for, in filling the gaps, the troops involved became trapped themselves. And yet, Kesselring stuck loyally to his duty as an officer and continued to do his best. Hitler and the OKW continually upset his plans.

"I was far too much a soldier not to know that I would not refuse to accept an opinion or to obey an order for which I was assured there were cogent reasons simply because I did not agree with it."[25]

By the end of March, Kesselring knew he must face the fact that the main part of his mission had not been accomplished. The Saar Palatinate had been lost, the bridgeheads at Remagen and Oppenheim were torn open and the Americans were pouring eastward and south.

The result of the Allied breakthrough caused the Germans to split their command. An Army Commander-in-Chief was assigned for the northwest and Kesselring became Commander-in-Chief Southwest along with assuming responsibility for the south and southeastern fronts. Thus, Italy was returned to his command as well as responsibility for the partisan war raging in Yugoslavia and the southern portion of the Soviet front.

By April, the only thing achievable was the buying of time for the German divisions engaged in the east, allowing them to fight their way back into the western zones.

In his autobiography, Kesselring devotes much space to his duty of saving the Germans from the Russians. He felt it was his absolute duty to save those German armies fighting in the east from falling into Soviet hands, "to give them time to fight their way back into the zones occupied by the Americans and British."[26]

Due to the squeezing of the front, German troops in a particular sector more than ever influenced the fate of those in another. This was the reason he gave for absolute intransigence in not allowing a separate surrender for any one sector of the various fighting fronts. He was convinced that should the armies in Italy be eliminated, it would spell the end of those in Bavaria and increase the danger for those remaining in the Balkans, just as disintegration of the front in south Germany would critically endanger other groups in the Alps, the southeast, southwest, and south. This became the driving philosophy he followed during the final days of the war.

"The primitive duty of comradeship made it impossible for the decent soldier to throw up the fighting knowing that his comrades were holding out in their last battle. It was unthinkable to surrender or abandon a position if it meant life or death to his fellows that he stand firm."[27]

The absolute duty for a German soldier was

not to allow Germans to fall into Russian hands. Because of this, he advocated fighting to the bitter end. That is the reason he refused to sanction a separate peace in Italy even though, since March, SS General Karl Wolff had been in close touch with Alan Dulles of the OSS in Switzerland, attempting to make a separate peace. Although as early as the Fall of 1944 Kesselring had approved just such a course of action, now, in 1945, he refused to allow it and even called for the arrest of Von Vietinghoff for endorsing Wolff's actions. Why was Kesselring allowing this useless slaughter to continue? The above quote from his autobiography answers that question, for it was indeed the absolute duty of the German soldier to fight on in order to save his fellow brothers-in-arms from falling into Soviet hands.

Macksey, in his excellent biography of Kesselring, reveals yet another insight into the latter's mind at the time. Mr. Macksey concluded that it was Kesselring's absolute loyalty to his oath to Hitler that made him refuse to approve any separate peace. Proof of this can be found in the fact that, within 36 hours of Hitler's death, Kesselring allowed the truce to take effect in Italy.

Kesselring's adopted son gives yet another interpretation. Kesselring held out, he said, in the hope that regardless of the Allied policy of unconditional surrender, should the Germans hold on, the Allies would eventually be forced to open negotiations on terms more tolerable for Germany. Perhaps it was all three interpretations that lend insight into this man at such a critical point in his military career.

With one week left to the war, Kesselring's headquarters had moved to the Alps, the last rallying point for Army Groups Southwest, Southeast, and parts of South. On May 6, his headquarters was the only one remaining in the Alps that had not yet surrendered. He then entered into communication with the Americans and finally capitulated. The war was over.

Although the hostilities had ceased, the trials of Field Marshal Albert Kesselring were just beginning. Sent from one prison after another, giving testimony and discussing with the American Historical Division, he awaited his own trial.

In 1947, Kesselring found himself returned to Italy, there to stand trial for war crimes. He was charged with two counts. The first charge against him was the shooting of the 335 Italians in the Ardeatine catacombs near Rome on March 24, 1944. Though his lawyer expertly demonstrated his innocence, Kesselring was pronounced guilty on the first count. The second count charged him with inciting, via two orders, his troops to murder civilians by way of reprisals for the actions of the Italian partisans. He was pronounced guilty of violating the laws and customs of hand warfare. The trial had lasted from February to May, 1947. The sentence was death by firing squad.

On July 4, 1947, Kesselring's death sentence was commuted to life imprisonment and in July, 1952, he emerged from prison a free man. He died on July 20, 1960.

Albert Kesselring shall forever be known and remembered as a master of prolonged defensive warfare, with few rivals in history. For two and one-half years, he fought the Allies from one stalemate to another by conducting incessant delaying actions against desperate odds. His allies, the Italians, turned against him and yet he was able to overcome this obstacle. He lost the trust of Hitler but his proven abilities finally restored that trust. He was virtually the only Commander-in-Chief who, after 1941, managed to change Hitler's way and survive. That in itself is deserving of the greatest of commendations.

Kesselring will also be remembered as an honorable man, one whose oath to his country meant as much as his life. He was a gentleman and a humanitarian. Thanks to him, many of the horrors of the SS were mitigated in their ferocity. That he was given the death sentence at this trial was a true travesty of justice. Because of Kesselring's efforts, many more civilian lives were saved. Due to his efforts, Rome, the Eternal City, garbed in its ancient splendor, is still able to sparkle for humanity. Were it not for Kesselring, this city could easily have been reduced to rubble. Florence, the great city of the Renaissance might also have been a casualty of war along with Pisa, home of the leaning tower. Both of these cities today might lie in ruin were it not for Kesselring's decisions.

We have many reasons to be grateful to Kesselring. We might however, say that if Kesselring were truly a humanitarian and cared for Italy, why didn't he retreat to the Alps as Rommel so forcefully advocated thereby eliminating war in Italy and not endangering its treasures. True, he could have, but we must also remember that there was one thing Albert Kesselring valued even more than the priceless treasures of Italy—Germany and his duty as a soldier.

SS! The very term evokes images of a loud knock on the door in the night followed by loved ones or entire families being dragged off by Black Uniformed thugs more commonly known as the Gestapo.

Still other images are of brutal, sadistic concentration camp guards burying piles of emaciated corpses or camp commandants ordering thousands of Jews, Slavs, and Russians to their death. These are probably the most vivid memories the modern world has of the organization known as the SS.

However, the SS was an all encompassing organization whose tenacles stretched into a variety of areas, each with their distinct but separate mission. Just as the Gestapo was unique from the Concentration Camp personnel, so too was the Waffen SS distinct from the others. It is this latter, or, to be more specific, one of its commanders to whom this chapter is devoted.

The original SS was but a small branch of the SA, Hitler's militant Nazi cronies more popularly referred to as the Brownshirts. The SS began as an elite cadre of exceptionally physically endowed young men, highly motived with the Nazi ideals, within the broad confines of the SA. This unit's primary function was to serve as actual or ceremonial bodyguards for the personage of Adolf Hitler, their Fuhrer, and were led by an ambitious and power hungry party up and comer, Heinrich Himmler.

As the SA continued to increase in size along with Hitler's power, they began to constitute a threat to the sanctity of the German Army. The latter was uncomfortable that another organization within the country was authorized to bear arms. Traditionally, the German Army held exclusive rights to this authority. It was well known that Rohm, nominal head of the SA desired the merger of his organization with the Army thereby creating a people's army with himself at its head. The German Generals were rightfully appalled that a condition such as this was allowed to exist at all and took Hitler to task for allowing it. Faced with a choice between the SA and the backing of the powerful Army, Hitler opted to cast his lot with the Generals. Execution squads from the SS purged the SA leadership as a sop to the Army and the organization, now leaderless, for all intents and purposes ceased to exist as a viable and influential unit. Himmler seized the opportunity to lay the foundation of his own private army and consolidate his power base. From the womb of this initial elite unit (Leibstandarte) sprang the Waffen SS.

Perhaps the most appropriate way to describe

the Waffen SS is to call it an army of the Nazi Party, not of Germany, for this is truly what it eventually evolved into.

Deeply steeped in the ideologies of National Socialism, this private army rose from the brigade sized Leibstandarte to eventually count in its ranks many divisions, corps, and even armies which were briefly the elite of the German armed forces and without doubt the most determined and toughest fighting units encountered by the Allies in Europe. Boasting such romantic sounding names as Das Reich, Tottenkopf, Germania and others, the Waffen SS units fought in every theatre and could be found where the fighting was the fiercest or most critical. For the bulk of the war, they were true shock troops. Later, as the manpower reserve dwindled in the wake of heavy casualties, foreigners sympathetic to the Nazi cause were induced to form their own Waffen SS divisions. These were appropriately named according to the country of origin; Waloon, Wiking, Nordland, etc.

The officers of the Waffen SS were, for the most part, former Army officers who had left the service for a variety of reasons ranging from incompetence to bona fide retirement. Attracted by the opportunity to once more serve in uniform, many of these were enticed into enlisting in the Waffen SS. Still others were favorites of Hitler or Himmler who were handed relatively important positions in the budding organization; Dietrich, Witt, and Lammerding are among the most notable. Of the former army officers, some rose to positions of high rank on merit and talent alone. Kurt Meyer and Felix Steiner are two of the most noteworthy of the latter. One Waffen SS General, however, had been a General in the Wehrmacht and, after a brief period of voluntary retirement, found that the urge to command troops was preferable to sitting idle, and so, offered his services to the Waffen SS. This man was former Lt. General Paul Hausser.

Paul Hausser was a typical German officer of the old school. Tall and imposing with sharply defined features dominated by a most prominent nose, he was once described by the American General Omar Bradley as "The ugliest man in uniform I have ever seen". This Brandenberger was born in 1880 to an Army officer and his wife and so was raised in Prussian Cadet Schools which no doubt accounted for his haughty and sarcastic manner. His early career in the army was unspectacular and routine. Although he had attended infantry school, staff college, and was a qualified General Staff officer, his career in WW I was uneventful as he was shifted to a variety of staff positions on both the Western and Eastern fronts. Von Seeckt, in his efforts to rebuild the German Army within the stringent and unreasonable confines of the Treaty of Versailles, desired that this new army retain as many General Staff officers as possible. Accordingly, Hausser was selected for inclusion in the small, 100,000 man army.

So Paul Hausser became part of that select group of officers selected to restore the German

Army to its former position of greatness and influence.

As the Army grew under the guiding hand of von Seeckt, so too grew the careers of many of the outstanding German Generals of WW II. Hausser, however, grew restless and tired of peace time soldiering and, after holding down a variety of staff positions, elected to take his retirement. His final command was that of Chief of Staff in Wehkries II. In January, 1932, during the period that Hitler's Nazis were growing in popularity and gaining gradual control of the country, Hausser retired with the rank of Lt. General.

Finding little else to do with his suddenly abundant free time, Hausser joined the German ex-soldiers association, Stahlhelm. Ernst Rohm, then one of Hitler's closest associates, absorbed the Stahlhelm into the SA via his efforts to become head of one people's army. Thus, as a member of this organization, Paul Hausser suddenly found himself a full fledged member of the Nazi Party. But there was little objection from the retired General for at that time, Hitler's brand of patriotism had yet to fully demonstrate its more offensive nature.

As Rohm began to further alienate Hitler, the latter become more open in his efforts to woo the German Generals to his support. Hitler was acutely aware that his dream of European domination could not become reality without the full support of the Army. Rohm had to go. The SA leader's vocal condemnation of Hitler's association with the German Army leadership provided the Fuhrer with the excuse he needed.

In June of 1934, during the notorious "Night of the Long Knives", the SA Leadership was totally eliminated and the way opened for the rise of the Waffen SS. Estimates of the number killed vary from between 90 to over 500, but one thing is certain, Himmler, always the opportunist, found the path open for his dreams of power and promptly proceeded to exploit the opportunity.

During the period of internal struggle within the Nazi hierarchy, Hausser had been induced to join the SS and was serving as an officer of Police during the Rohm purge. Once Himmler realized that the shackles had been cast off and he now had a relatively free hand, plans were made to take advantage of Hausser's training and background.

As the highest ranking former Army officer in the SS, Hausser now became invaluable. Like Rohm, Himmler too sought to be head of his own private army. The difference was that Himmler was a bit more discreet than the outspoken and vocal Rohm. Also, Himmler, in 1934, held few illusions about replacing the Reichswehr as the military arm of the Third Reich. However, in order to have the SS taken seriously as a military formation, certain steps would be necessary.

Early in 1935, the first SS cadet schools were founded at Bad Tolz and Brunswick. The intent of these schools was to provide formal training for budding SS officers and were absolutely essential if the SS was to become a true fighting organization. The obvious choice to head this educational process was Paul Hausser. He related:

> "I considered that the SS force must be formed on the well tried training regulations of the Reichswehr."[1]

The SS now began an intense program of expansion and under Hausser's tutelage, started to take shape as a viable military unit. Small cadres were consolidated, trained until eventually, three regiment sized units existed. In 1936, Hausser was promoted to the equivalent of Major General and given overall command of the SS formations. Dietrich, commander of the Leibstandarte, objected strenuously to taking orders from a former Army officer but at Himmler's insistence, gradually acceded.

Despite his role in shaping the SS, Hausser refused to accept the attitude that he was strictly a party soldier and had little desire to accept the political ideology irrevocably entwined with his fledgling army. His only desire at that time was to be a General commanding troops. As the senior member of the SS, he would soon realize this goal.

As Hitler maneuvered Germany closer to war, Hausser continued to devote his attention to the training and molding of his regiments into combat troops. At his urging, Waffen SS units were finally assigned to active duty with the Army. The first units were attached to General Werner Kempff's division and Hausser went along as liaison officer to the army divisional staff. With this step, he left behind forever, administrative duties.

The Waffen SS units were relegated to a secondary role during the initial stages of the Battle for France. The second stage of the battle however, saw the participation of the first SS Division molded from the regiments, Germania, Der Fuhrer, and Deutschland. This division followed in the wake of von Kleist's panzers in pursuit of the reeling French. On June 17, a strong French force attempted to break through on Hausser's front to avoid being encircled. Hausser's soldiers threw back the French effort and the SS troops captured over 30,000 prisoners. As a result, SS troops finally gained a small measure of acceptance as combat soldiers. Hausser's army experience had paid off as proven by the fact that his units had suffered fewer casualties than some of his contemporaries in the Wehrmacht.

The period following the fall of France was one of continued growth and training for the men of the Waffen SS. As a result of the successful baptism of fire in France, Hitler authorized the expansion of the Waffen SS. The makings of an SS Army began to take shape.

Operation Barbarossa, the German invasion of Russia, began in June of 1941. Das Reich division under Hausser's command, found itself part of von Vietinghoff's XLVI Corps in Panzer Group Guderian. This panzer group charged headlong into enemy country, chewing off huge hunks of Soviet real estate in a spectacular and unprecedented advance through the very heart of mother Russia; objective—Moscow. The SS units performed magnificently and soon earned the unqualified praise of Guderian. The latter had nought but praise for Hausser and after observing Das Reich in action, rated its commander clear headed and talented. High praise for sure from such an illustrious General.

Das Reich participated in virtually all of Guderian's great victories including the bitter fighting around Yelna and the bloody battles around Bordino where no quarter was given and both sides suffered heavily. Early on October 15, Paul Hausser was as usual up early and visiting his front line units. As they prepared to jump off for an attack, Hausser's group came under fire from Soviet artillery. Members of the party were killed and/or severely wounded. Included on the casualty list of that day was the name of General Paul Hausser. A piece of shrapnel had buried itself in his face causing irreparable damage to one eye. Although he was invalided home. Hausser was determined not to let the loss of an eye deter his career.

As early as August, 1941, Hausser had urged Hitler to allow the SS units to incorporate armour into their formations. The swift defeat of France and the initial successes in Russia had made a lasting impression. The Fuhrer, flushed with victory and justifiably proud of his SS troops, decided to grant Hausser's request.

The Wehrmacht Generals received this news with mixed emotions. Many of them cast wary glances at Himmler's army as it increased in size and strength. Objections were raised to the building of new formations when replacements were urgently required on the Eastern front. In addition, the SS seemed to attract the cream of the enlistments leaving its rejects available for service with the regular army.

On the other hand, many field commanders were more than happy to have the SS units serving under them. Although the SS formations considered themselves above army discipline and were difficult to handle at times, they fought with their own brand of elan and determination bordering on the fanatic and consistently gave a good account of themselves.

In the middle of 1942, Hitler authorized formation of the first SS Corps as a prelude of things to come. The obvious choice to command this Corps was Paul Hausser and he was duly appointed over the heads of party hacks commanding other SS formations.

The formation of the I SS Panzer Corps was considered a triumph for Himmler and the Nazi Party. With his request for armour granted as well, Hausser set about reequipping his units and retraining them. They would shortly find themselves earning their reputation.

The Russian offensive at Stalingrad and further north had threatened the existence of the entire German Southern front. In mid January, Hausser's SS Panzer Corps, redesignated II SS Panzer Corps, was ordered to join Army Group B in the Ukraine.

As the Russian pressure against Army Group B continued to increase in intensity, II SS Panzer Corps was committed to the defense of the Ukrainian capitol of Kharkov.

February, 1943, was a critical time for the German Army in the East. Stalingrad had fallen and the entire weight of the Soviet Army in the Ukraine was now turned against Manstein's newly created Army Group Don. Faced with the responsibility of protecting the rear of First Panzer Army in the Caucasus, Army Group Don itself faced the prospect of being totally cut off from its neighbor to the North, Army Group B.

As the Russians drove a wedge between the two Army Groups, strong pressure was brought against the city of Kharkov. Responsibility for defense of this city rested in the hands of Paul Hausser and his II SS Panzer Corps. The Corps was made up of two well tried and tested divisions, Das Reich and Leibstandarte.

Hitler was notorious for demanding that no step backward be allowed to take place. Accordingly, he ordered that Kharkov be held at all costs. The Fuhrer was supremely confident that his orders would be obeyed to the letter, for after all, wasn't Kharkov being defended by loyal SS troops?

Manstein, however, was eager to have the Russians continue their southward thrust so that their spearheads could be severed and the attack thrown back with heavy loss.

II SS Panzer Corps was under the overall command of Army Detachment Lanz who reported up the ladder to Army Group B. Hausser's subsequent action would serve to deceive the Russians into thinking that total victory was imminent.

On February 11, Hitler was still raging about the tragedy of Stalingrad. He demanded the OKW signal Lanz that at all costs, Kharkov was to be held. At this point, the city was virtually surrounded by Soviet troops and Hausser and his beleaguered formations were entrenched inside the city. There was only one thing certain to Hausser at this time; he would call the shots, not someone hundreds of miles in the rear.

As the Russians began to squeeze the pocket around Kharkov, Hausser hung on grimly. His days were spent visiting his units, sizing up the situation at the front line, followed by a return to his headquarters to pour over situation maps and consult with his staff. The street fighting in the city reached intense proportions as the Russians infiltrated and continued to apply the pressure. Although the SS troops were making the Russians pay dearly for every inch of ground, the attrition was more than Hausser could reasonably afford.

On February 13, Hitler reiterated his order to Lanz that under no circumstances was Kharkov to be abandoned. Lanz was not prepared to disobey Hitler and, after adding his endorsement to the order, forwarded it on to Hausser.

By the next day, the encirclement of Kharkov was almost complete. Hausser requested authorization from Lanz for a breakout to the west. The latter refused to contradict Hitler's express orders and quickly denied permission. By this time, the situation had become critical. Hausser's entry in his log read:

"Enemy facing Kharkov's eastern and northeastern front greatly strengthened on 14.2 Attacks along Chugeyev and Volchansk roads repulsed by last reserves. Enemy penetration eight miles deep near southern airfield as far as Osnova. Mopping up now in progress but with inadequate forces. No forces available for sealing off enemy penetration north-west of Kharkov, at Grossdeutschland Division. All offensive troops tied down in the south for the moment. 320th Infantry Division not yet absorbed into main defensive line. Its condition according to general staff reports, precludes offensive employment for a few days.

"Inside Kharkov mob firing at troops and vehicles. No forces available for mopping up since everything in front line. City, including railway, stores, and ammunition dumps, effectively dynamited at Army orders. City burning. Systematic withdrawal increasingly improbable each day. Assumptions underlying Kharkov's strategic importance no longer valid. Request renewed Fuhrer decision whether Kharkov to be defended to the last man."[2]

Despite Lanz's unequivocal refusal to authorize a retreat, Hausser was not one to stand idly by and watch his command frittered away in pursuit of a senseless endeavor. Back at his headquarters, Hitler was supremely confident that his demands would be carried out to the last letter, for, were not the SS troops the most loyal in all of Germany? Perhaps they were, but their commander refused to sacrifice these brave warriors in quest of symbolic gestures. His long army career had instilled in the man a high degree of common sense tempered by coolness under fire and the ability to exercise clear judgment in time of crisis.

Shortly after noon on February 15, Hausser informed Lanz's headquarters that he was issuing orders for an evacuation of the city. Lanz wired back immediately:

"Kharkov will be defended under all circumstances."[3]

General Lanz was not prepared to disobey a direct order from Hitler.

Fortunately for the SS formations, their commander was made of sterner stuff. Lanz's order was completely ignored as Hausser's foremost concern was the extradition of his corps from certain disaster. He therefore assumed full responsibility for disobeying a direct Fuhrer order and was prepared to suffer the consequences at a later date. During the afternoon, astride a tank, Paul Hausser led his troops out of Kharkov with the Russians licking at their heels. II SS Panzer Corps would live to fight another day.

Ironically, when word was received at Fuhrer headquarters that Kharkov had been abandoned, it was not Hausser who felt the fury of Hitler's wrath. The unfortunate General Lanz was sacked and his command dissolved.

The evacuation of Kharkov lulled the Russian High Command into a false sense of victory. Surely, they believed, if the vaunted SS units were in full retreat, then the entire German Army on the southern front must be in general retreat all along the front. Unfortunately for them, Hausser's actions had served only to husband his forces for another crack at his antagonists. Playing right into Manstein's hands, the Russians now began their advance to the Black Sea in earnest. As far as Stalin was concerned, Army Group Don including First and Fourth Panzer Armies and Seventeenth Army along with various army detachments, were now ripe for destruction. This erroneous assumption on the part of the Russians could not have been more beneficial to Manstein's plans.

The recovery of the Southern front has already been related in detail in the chapter on Field Marshal von Manstein. To say that it was a miraculous recovery would be an understatement at best. One detail of the counteroffensive

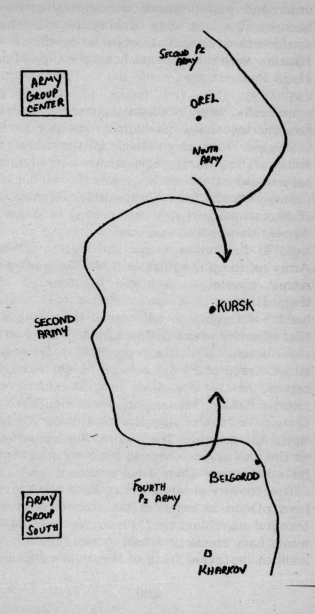

ARMY GROUP CENTER

SECOND Pz ARMY

OREL

NINTH ARMY

SECOND ARMY

KURSK

FOURTH Pz ARMY

BELGORODD

ARMY GROUP SOUTH

KHARKOV

launched by the Germans is worthy of note, however. The left wing of Manstein's brilliant counteroffensive was spearheaded by the II SS Panzer Corps under the redoubtable Paul Hausser.

Slashing into the flanks of the Soviet spearheads, the SS tankers attacked with a ferocity that knew no bounds, spurred on by their anxiety to exact revenge for the debacle at Kharkov. The Russian spearheads were blunted, severed from the main body, and thrown back in disorder with heavy casualties. Manstein's counterstroke had not only proved brilliant in concept, it was well executed.

As II SS Panzer Corps and Fourth Panzer Army rolled up the Russian front, the spectre of Kharkov once again began to loom on the horizon.

With the enemy in full retreat, the possibility that Kharkov would change hands for the fourth time became a distinct possibility. However, Army Group plans did not call for the outright capture of the city itself but instead, recommended flanking movements North and South of the city with the objective of cutting off the Soviet units within. The prospect for a continuation of the advance beyond Kharkov was slight for the Spring thaw was imminent and the danger of overextending the flanks of Army Group Don was foremost in the minds of Army Group staff. Therefore, Hausser decided that he would have ample time to seek retribution.

On the outboard flank of Manstein's counter--

offensive, II SS Panzer Corps was directed to outflank Kharkov to the West, gain a position north of the city, and invest it on a West to East axis. Hausser set off with his units in a great semi-circular route designed to achieve his designated objective. Meanwhile, Fourth Panzer Army under Col. General Hermann Hoth, attempting to outflank the city from the south, ran afoul of a spirited and determined Soviet defense and lost their momentum. Once more, Hausser took the initiative on his own and charged down from the North, blasted his way into and through the city, and took the Soviet units facing Hoth in the rear. On March 13, Kharkov was once more officially declared German and the Swastika was hoisted in Red Square. For Hausser and the II SS Panzer Corps, revenge was sweet. Unfortunately, just as forecast, the Spring thaw set in, bringing with it the miles and miles of impassable mud that thwarted any effort to resume the offensive. The Germans now stood on the lines previously held. A large Soviet bulge protruding into the German lines around Kursk was all the Red Army had to show for almost six months of continuous attack. Kharkov, however, would prove to be the final German offensive victory in the East.

To even the amateur, it was obvious that the Kursk salient poised a threat to the German front and required elimination before a further Eastward advance could be contemplated. Unfortunately, both sides were acutely aware of this fact.

Operation Citadel, the Battle of Kursk, has been examined and reexamined as a classic confrontation of armour on a large scale; of the irresistible force against the immovable object. For a thorough examination of the battle, an entire volume would be necessary.

Indecision within the ranks of the leading German commanders delayed a decision on Kursk and allowed the Russians enough breathing space to heavily fortify the bulge with massive defensive positions, their best troops, ample reserves, and their finest commanders. By the time the Germans finally made up their minds to eliminate the Kursk bulge and set a date for the attack, the Russians had built a veritable impenetrable front.

Representing Manstein's Army Group, Fourth Panzer Army under the very able and competent Hoth, was to attack from the South in conjunction with another attack on the Northern side of the bulge by General Walther Model's Ninth Army. II SS Panzer Corps was incorporated into the Fourth Panzer Army and positioned in the center of the line flanked by XLVIII Panzer Corps with 3 panzer divisions on the left under General von Knobelsdorff and Army Detachment Kempf on the far right whose two panzer divisions were directed to provide flanking cover for Hausser.

For the coming offensive, Hausser would have under command Leibstandarte, Totenkopf, and Das Reich. 8 of Germany's finest divisions aligned abreast covering a stretch of just under 40 miles.

Prior to the launching of the attack an order was passed to the tank crews that underscored the heavy emphasis the Germans were placing on the battle:

"In no circumstances will tanks be stopped to render assistance to those which have been disabled. Recovery is the responsibility of engineer units only. Tank commanders are to press on to their objective as long as they retain mobility. Where a tank is rendered immobile but the gun is in working order, the crew will continue to give fire support from a static position."[4]

General von Mellenthin, Chief-of-Staff of XVLIII Panzer Corps added this comment:

"Never had there been a major combat operation that could have been better prepared than this one."[5]

Early on the morning of July 5, the massive concentration of Russian artillery got the jump on the Germans and opened fire on the Wehrmacht assembly areas, taking the Germans completely by surprise. It was a full two hours later before the German artillery could recover enough to return the fire. Then, the heavy field guns of both armies engaged in a fierce, point blank duel.

The magnificent German talent for organization now began to pay dividends and their recuperative powers proved superb. However, the Russian barrage had accomplished its goal and threw the German timetable off schedule. Everything in view was ablaze as fields and villages burned and roaring aircraft flew overhead leaving death and destruction in their wake.

Despite a determined resistance, Hausser's units managed to break through the first line of Soviet resistance within a few hours. Tank losses though were high and the Russian fire was able to take a heavy toll of the following infantry. The entire Russian defensive system was ribboned with deep, zigzagging trenches that, when once the tanks had passed, special squads of hand-picked Russian soldiers rose from these trenches and operated in the rear of the advancing Wehrmacht formations making it difficult to support the advancing panzers.

By noon of the following day, the SS armoured wedges of Ferdinands and Tigers serving as an axe crashed deeper and deeper into the Russian defensive zone and managed a 20 mile deep penetration. The Soviet Sixth Guards Army was shattered by the determined SS troopers. Through this breach, Hausser moved the might of his entire corps which then fanned out behind the Russian positions. Once more the tried and true tactics of the glory days of the Blitzkrieg were dusted off and used. But the deeper they advanced, the more the infantry became scattered as the resistance became heavier. To the left, Knobelsdorff's formations found themselves

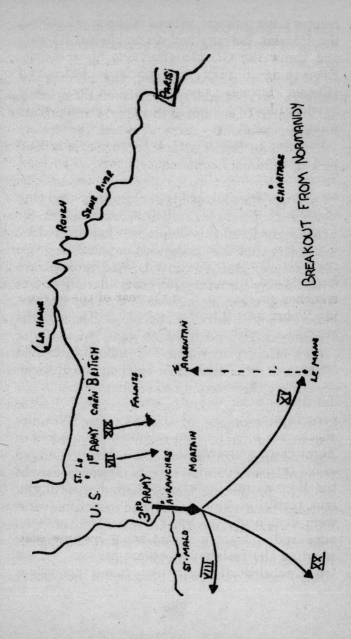

BREAKOUT FROM NORMANDY

unable to keep pace with Hausser's units and the flanks of the SS spearheads became dangerously exposed.

As they continued forward, the Ferdinands, the great weapon which had delayed the opening of Citadel until enough of them and the Panthers became available, now proved extremely vulnerable to Soviet attack because of a critical lack of secondary armament.

"They were incapable of close-range fighting since they lacked sufficient ammunition for their guns and this defect was aggravated by the fact that they possessed no machine guns. Once they (the Ferdinands) had broken into the enemy's infantry zone they literally had to go quail shooting with cannon. They did not manage to neutralize, let alone destroy, the enemy rifles and machine guns, so that our own infantry was unable to follow up behind them. By the time they reached the Russian artillery they were on their own."[6]

On the morning of July 7, the SS units stormed Butovo putting the Soviet defenders to flight. Full of confidence, the Germans surged forward. Soviet reinforcements, however, caught up with the fleeing troops, halted their flight, wheeled them about, dug in, and met the advancing panzers head on. The Germans were stopped cold. By evening, both sides found themselves fighting bitterly for individual hills.

The battlefront soon became an incohesive

fighting line as fierce duels erupted in most sectors. At dawn of the next day, the fighting continued without ebb. The Russians, reacting slowly but deliberately, were satisfied that they were causing the Germans to bleed profusely. In some areas, the Soviet armour could be seen perched atop hills overlooking the battlefield where they were able to blast the panzers at will.

The German drive began to peter out and come apart at the seams. Even though Hausser's units continued to advance at a snail's pace, the supporting units on either side of II SS Panzer Corps bogged down. Von Mellenthin realized that the back of the German attack had finally been broken.

"Experience shows that the Russian soldier has an almost incredible ability to stand up to the heaviest artillery fire and air-bombardment while the Russian command remains unmoved by the bloodiest losses caused by shelling and bombs and ruthlessly adheres to its preconceived plans."[7]

By July 9, after 5 days of brutal fighting, Fourth Panzer Army had registered small gains but at a prohibitive cost in men and equipment. Not only were they still 55 miles from Kursk, but 90 miles short of a linkup with Model's Ninth Army attacking the northern side of the bulge.

Midnight of the same day found the battle still raging. Hausser was incredibly still moving forward slowly and had smashed the Soviet First Tank Army in addition to the aforementioned Sixth Guards. The fighting continued to blaze back and forth for the next few days with neither side gaining the upper hand.

July 12 was the day of the great tank battle. Both German and Russian units alike prepared for an all-out assault that day. For Hoth's Fourth Panzer Army, it was to be an all out effort to capture the town of Oboyan. For the Russians, it was now time for the counteroffensive to begin.

Their old antagonist from Moscow, Leningrad, and Stalingrad was in overall command of the Kursk salient. Marshal Georgi Zhukov' had allowed the Germans to advance just far enough to bleed themselves white against his brilliantly designed defensive perimeters. The Germans had accommodated him and had indeed bled and, now that they had shot their bolt and worn themselves out, the time for counteraction was ripe.

Of all the German forces involved in Operation Citadel, Hausser's Corps had achieved the most and made the deepest penetration. Therefore, they posed the most immediate threat to the Russians. Shortly after daybreak, wave after wave of Russian bombers and ground attack planes pounded the German lines concentrating on Leibstandarte, Totenkopf, and Das Reich. General Romistrov's tank force, containing 850 tanks, most of them the formidable T-34, began to roll and shortly spotted their quarry; the 700 tanks of II SS Panzer Corps.

In a very brief space of time, the battlefield was turned into a scene out of Dante's inferno—choked with large clouds of dust, boiling smoke, aircraft flying blindly and no one able to distinguish friend from foe.

In this great tank clash, the Russians held the advantage of the higher ground. The T-34's charged the Germans who elected to use their more heavily armoured tanks in an artillery duel—their guns against the Russians—but this advantage was neutralized by the wild charge of the Soviet tanks which managed to find the German flank.

The duel lasted for over eight hours of exploding blazing tanks. Shells and guns blasted in an ever rising crescendo, louder and louder, drowning out the screams of human flesh caught in the horror of crashing and exploding steel. Finally, the Russian cavalry type charge broke the back of the Germans.

"We found ourselves taking on a seemingly inexhaustible mass of enemy armour—never have I received such an overwhelming impression of Russian strength and numbers as on that day. The clouds of dust made it difficult to get help from the Luftwaffe, and soon many of the T-34's had broken past our screen and were streaming like rats over the battlefield."[8]

Finally, the battle dissolved into small groups of tanks fighting tanks. By nightfall, the battlefield was once more completely ablaze. The weary, battle fatigued SS troops thought that surely hell was like Kursk.

Although on the surface the great tank battle appeared to be a standoff, the Soviets were in fact the true victors for, in retrospect, the duel of July 12 had finally destroyed the ability of the Germans to dictate where and when the offensives would take place. Their initiative was irrevocably lost. Kursk truly marked the death knell of the vaunted German Panzer arm.

On July 17, Citadel was officially called off. Hitler justified his termination of the battle with the excuse that divisions were required for the Balkans and Italy and the only place they were available was on the Eastern Front.

The SS formations had earned the grudging respect of their Wehrmacht colleagues. At Kharkov and Kursk they had fought bitterly and incurred high casualties but acquitted themselves magnificently. The enemy was fully aware of the fighting caliber of the SS divisions as witnessed by the fact that at Kursk, the main weight of the Russian counterattack was concentrated against Hausser's corps. In spite of the overwhelming and well laid out defensive system, II SS Panzer Corps had achieved a deeper penetration into the salient than any other Wehrmacht formation.

One of Hitler's first orders upon terminating Operation Citadel was to order II SS Panzer Corps transferred to France. This order was quickly modified and it was a number of weeks before the SS formations finally found themselves travelling West.

The winter of 1943–44 was spent in the relative peace of occupied France. II SS Panzer Corps was rested and the tremendous losses incurred at Kursk were made good. Thanks to the performance of Hausser's corps, Hitler authorized the creation of another SS Panzer Corps. Thus the I SS Panzer Corps was raised and placed under the command of the Fuhrer's old party comrade, Joseph Sepp-Dietrich. The latter was hardly the caliber of soldier that Hausser was, but he was a favorite at court and a symbol of Nazism. Probably the most appropriate description of Dietrich's ability is contained in the words of Field Marshal von Rundstedt. When discussing various commanders just prior to the Battle of the Bulge, he said of Dietrich, "the man is decent but stupid."

While the II SS Panzer Corps was refitting under the watchful eye of the all observant Hausser, the situation in the East continued to deteriorate. From Kursk onward, the Germans were unable to regain the initiative. In the face of incessant Soviet attacks, the German Army in the East was forced back, step by step, mile by mile, while Hitler raged and stormed against his generals and continued to deny them permission to conduct strategic withdrawals and effectively hindering their flexibility. Great yawning gaps were torn between Army Groups and between individual armies within those groups. The most dangerous situation continued to exist in the area of Manstein's Army Group where the Red Army continued to visualize the isolation and destruction of all the German forces on the Southern front. The Winter battles in the great Dnieper bend were in keeping with this concept.

In March the situation became critical. Vaututin's and Zhukov's constant pressure had finally born fruit and a deep wedge was driven between First and Fourth Panzer Armies. In the ensuing battles, the German front was pierced in numerous areas and pressed against the Carpathian Mountains. Hube's First Panzer Army was shortly cut off and completely surrounded east of the Dneister River. Supplied by air, the 7 German divisions in this army hung on until late in March when ordered by Manstein to break out to the west.

The Russians continued to apply the pressure and three tank armies drove south on Hube's left flank. In the first week of April, Fourth Panzer Army began an attack in an endeavor to link up with the divisions of Hube trying to break out to the West. Spearheading this attack was II SS Panzer Corps under Hausser recently recalled from France. Through the mud and snow, Hausser's divisions attacked with grim ferocity. The strength of the German attack took the Russians completely by surprise and Hausser maintained the pressure, refusing to let the enemy catch their breath. On April 6, leading elements of Hausser's corps linked up with the advance units of First Panzer Army at Buchach and opened a narrow corridor through which the retreating units of First Panzer Army streamed westward in the largest breakout of the war. After this battle, known as the Battle of Tarnapol, the Southern front stabilized itself to some extent as Model, who had replaced Manstein during the last week in March, managed to form a solid front. Once more the II SS Panzer Corps was pulled out of line and this time sent to Poland. Hausser's sternest test was yet to come.

On June 6, 1944, the Western Allies under Eisenhower landed in Normandy and quickly gained a foothold on the continent. Although confined to the Normandy area, they continued their buildup until such time as adequate strength became available for a breakout into France proper. It was soon apparent that the Allied containment would burst at the seams from sheer size alone. The Germans knew that their hold on France was tenuous. But Hitler was determined to hang on and dispatched everything he could lay his hands on to the threatened front. Included in the reinforcements rushed to Normandy was the II SS Panzer Corps from Poland.

The Allies soon found themselves caught in a desperate slugging match. Step by step, mile by bloody mile, they slowly advanced through the hedgerows of Normandy despite a skillful and tenacious defense by the German Seventh Army. Each yard of ground was bitterly contested as the Germans took full advantage of the natural barriers established over the centuries. Seventh Army's commander, General Dollman had led this Army from the time it settled down to occupation duty after the fall of France. Suddenly, he found himself burdened with the ever present danger of an Allied breakout. The sudden pressure proved too much for Dollman's health. On June 28, General Friedrich Dollman suffered a massive heart attack and died at his headquarters. By this time, Hitler had become increasingly disenchanted with his generals and so tabbed a loyal SS General to replace Dollman. Paul Hausser became the first General of the SS to command an entire army.

Hausser found himself facing the might of the American Army under General Omar Bradley and responsible for containing this force within the restrictive confines of the Cotentin Peninsula. During the last week in July, Bradley launched Operation Cobra designed to force a breakout into metropolitan France. On July 30, Avranches at the base of the Peninsula and the gateway to France was blown open by the Americans. Now Bradley authorized the activation of Patton's Third Army and prepared to exploit the breakthrough. Patton quickly thrust three Corps through the opening at Avranches.

Hitler took one look at the advance of Patton and immediately sensed a golden opportunity. Once more one of the Fuhrer's grandiose schemes would spell disaster for the German Army. Hausser was ordered to attack Patton's flank and cut Third Army off from its base of supply. Despite all obvious evidence to the contrary, Hitler was confident of an overwhelming

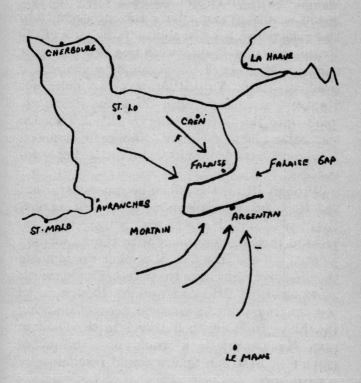

THE FALAISE GAP
AUGUST 1944

victory. The German commanders in the field, however, were stunned. Complete Allied domination of the skies over France prohibited mass movement of units and Hausser knew that he would be unable to muster sufficient strength to stem the Allied tide. In addition, the bulk of the Panzer units in France were tied down further north holding back Montgomery's British in front of Caen. To withdraw these units for Hausser's use would open the gates for an advance into the German rear by the British. On the other hand, without armoured support, Hausser's attack would have little hope for success.

Through Ultra, the Allies became aware that the Germans were planning an attack against Bradley's front. Hausser and Kluge* both expressed their disagreement with the attack and pointed out that the lack of armour would doom the offensive right from the outset. Furthermore, as experienced field commanders they were all too conscious of the consequences of allowing the Allies to make their way into the German rear. Hausser's attack would be a desperate gamble at best and failure would result in dire consequences.

Hitler refused to be swayed. Of course he could not be aware of the strength of the magnificently equipped and fresh units of the American Army. The loyal Hausser, having witnessed first-hand

*Field Marshal Gunther von Kluge replaced von Rundstedt as Commander-in-Chief West.

the consequences of Hitler's stand fast orders on the Eastern front, now began to have reservations about Hitler's ability to handle the war. Surely it was sheer madness to launch an all out offensive against an enemy superior in all ways, and to do it without adequate aerial support. Nevertheless, although Hausser was not adverse to disobeying direct orders (witness Kharkov), he made up his mind to go ahead with the attack fully aware of the ramifications.

For the attack, Hitler decided to support Hausser with armour withdrawn from Panzer Group West in front of Caen. In honor of the occasion, he created another force from these units and designated it Fifth Panzer Army. Sepp-Dietrich, left to his own devices in front of Caen, protested bitterly and called it madness. He too began to waver in his unilateral support of Hitler.

Hausser wanted to launch the attack immediately and informed Kluge of his decision. Unfortunately, Hitler had other plans and ordered Kluge to delay the start of the offensive until more of Patton's units moved through the corridor. In this way, a successful German attack would prove more costly to the Americans.

Finally, on August 8, Hausser received permission to launch his attack. But, on the same day, the American XV Corps under General Wade Haislip reached LeMans, deep on the flank of Seventh Army. The same day, Montgomery launched an all out offensive at Caen.

Hausser and Eberbach, commander of Fifth

Panzer Army knew that they were sticking their heads into the jaws of a possible giant pincer but dutifully launched the attack. Allied air power thwarted Hausser's attack from the beginning as units moving forward were harassed during every daylight hour and severely mauled. Units were unable to reach their designated start positions and became separated and scattered. By the time Seventh Army, or what was left of it, reached the jumping off line, it was grievously understrength and Army communications was severely disrupted. The attack never did gain sufficient momentum.

Adding to the woes of Seventh Army was an attack launched on its right flank by the American VII and XIX Corps under Generals Collins and Corlett. With most of its strength concentrated in the spearheads of the attack, the very last thing that Seventh Army was prepared to handle was a heavy attack against its right flank. Two days after the beginning Mortain offensive, Hausser besieged Kluge; "Call the damn thing off!"

Meanwhile, Montgomery's units at Caen finally managed to penetrate the weakened German defensive ring around Caen and struck out for Falaise, the Canadians in the van.

When Haislip reached LeMans, Patton saw that the Germans had presented him with an unprecedented opportunity. He immediately urged Bradley and Montgomery to allow him to wheel XV Corps around and send it to Argentan to await the Canadians making for Falaise.

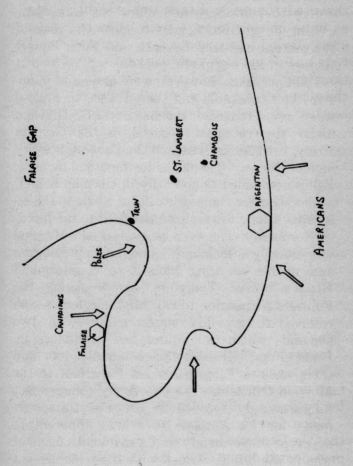

As Kluge's Mortain offensive stalled and lost what little momentum it had managed to generate, Haislip set off for Argentan but with orders to halt there and allow the Canadians coming down from Falaise to close the jaws of the pincers and trap Seventh and Fifth Panzer Armies inside a gigantic pocket.

The Canadians, however, were unable to maintain their timetable and the advance to Falaise was slow. A tenacious defense by 12 SS Division under the youngest General in the German Army, Kurt Meyer, resisted the Canadians every inch of the way. Thanks to his fanatical defense, Falaise remained temporarily in German hands.

Shortly after Hausser's call for a halt to the offensive, Kluge too realized the peril to his forces in Normandy. The ever cautious Field Marshal was nobody's fool and found himself hedging and unable to bring himself to countermand Hitler's orders. Therefore, before asking the Fuhrer's permission to call off the offensive, he resolved to have his request endorsed by two Generals whom the Fuhrer had confidence in. Hausser and Eberbach were requested to add their voice to Kluge's request for a halt to the Mortain Offensive. The two Army commanders unhesitatingly acceded to Kluge's strange request for, by August 10, it was apparent to everyone in Normandy that a mammoth disaster was in the offing. Armed with the endorsement of the two loyal Nazi Generals, Kluge's courage was bolstered and he forwarded his recommendations to Berlin.

Two days later, on August 12, Haislip rolled into Argentan. After pushing a reconnaissance in force on towards Falaise, he was promptly ordered to withdraw, hold his ground at Argentan, and allow Montgomery to close the pocket. Haislip was appalled. On his left stood two entire German armies. A rapid linkup with the Canadians would result in a victory rivalling that of Stalingrad.

On August 14, Hitler answered the pleas of his generals. The offensive must continue. Hausser considered it sheer madness and simply ignored the order. In fact, by this time, he had no alternative. The rapidly developing pocket around his formations had shrunk so that the Americans were able to direct artillery fire into the pocket from three sides.

Kluge went forward into the pocket to meet with his commanders and gain a first-hand impression of the situation. Enroute, Allied fire destroyed his command vehicle and with it, his radio, so that the unfortunate Field Marshal lost all contact with his headquarters for a number of crucial hours. Hitler would eventually be led to believe that Kluge's disappearance was due to the fact that the latter was seeking contact with the Allies in order to arrange for a surrender.

Despite the heavy concentration of Allied fire, Kluge did manage to locate the individual headquarters of his two army commanders and reiterate his refusal to authorize a withdrawal without the express consent of Hitler. The two Generals could not have obeyed even if they were willing to. It was simply an impossible order to carry out.

Finally, the following day, a reluctant Hitler gave his permission for a withdrawal to begin. He had finally realized that his stubbornness would, if continued, write off two entire German armies. With these orders in hand, Kluge finally ordered Hausser and Eberbach to start withdrawing their units. He need not have bothered. The Allied pressure had become so intensive that both armies were being pushed back all along the line and the two commanders really had little choice in the matter.

Meanwhile, Meyer's youthful SS troops were struggling desperately to repulse wave after wave of Canadian attacks but it was obvious that a breakthrough was simply a matter of time. The fanatical Meyer was painfully aware that only his troops stood in the way of the Canadians reaching Falaise and springing the trap shut on Hausser and Eberbach. On August 16, while personally directing his division, Meyer was struck in the head by a piece of shrapnel. With his wounding, some of the spirit went out of the defense.

Inside the pocket it was a slaughter. Allied fire from all directions exacted a terrible toll. Men and animals alike were caught in a dreadful hail of fire and steel that tore apart bodies, blasted eardrums, shattered minds, and made the earth tremble. The heavy German reliance on horse drawn transport created havoc as dead animals and burning vehicles clogged roads. All telephone links between various units had long ceased to exist, having been blasted apart by American artillery. Hausser was reduced to personally travelling to each unit to issue orders for its positioning to effectively cover the withdrawal. His only concern now was to get as many troops as possible out of the pocket. Equipment was abandoned as the Germans had but one thought in mind; make for the rapidly closing exit between Falaise and Argentan.

On August 17, Field Marshal Walther Model arrived in France with orders to replace Kluge. After a quick glance at the situation maps, he ordered II SS Panzer Corps under Bittrich to halt the British advance at Trun. The Germans were straining desperately to hold open both sides of the rapidly shrinking pocket.

The entire narrow escape corridor was within point blank range of Allied artillery fire. In addition, rocket firing Typhoons ranged at will, taking a terrible toll of life as men and animals streamed eastward through the corridor of death. Vehicles were useless as any movement along the road attracted the attention of the Typhoons. The Allied pilots dubbed the escape route "The Killing Ground".

By August 19, only a 3 mile wide corridor remained open between Chambois and St. Lambert. Hausser ordered the injured Meyer to hold the Canadians out of the former and keep the escape route open at all cost. He then set off himself to lead one group of survivors to safety.

All semblance of order had ceased to exist.

Every divisional and corps staff was on the road with but one thought in mind. Escape! Meyer's valiant stand on the shoulder of the pocket at Chambois, although brief, gave the retreating Germans a brief respite. Despite the efforts of 12 SS Division, near midnight of the 19th, Chambois fell. But, spurred on by panic, the retreating Germans overran the thin Canadian and Polish screen by sheer weight alone. Kurt Meyer described this experience:

> "As though rocket-propelled, we rushed through the astonished infantry in a few seconds and in a silence broken only by the bursting of a few shells."[9]

Streaming blood from his reopened wound, Kurt Meyer made his way out of the pocket.

General Elfeldt, commander of LXXXIV Corps was not as fortunate. Leading a small group of staff officers, he was captured by Polish troops as he attempted to make his way out of the pocket. Eberbach was more fortunate. Cut off from his units, he led a small group of infantry through to safety on foot.

The commander of II Parachute Corps, General Meindl reached the wall of the pocket early on August 20. There he made contact with Hausser and, after conferring briefly, the two parted to make their separate way to safety. Shortly afterward, an artillery shell exploded near Hausser and severely wounded the Seventh

Army commander. All contact with him was lost.

As small groups of troops streamed out of the pocket and made their way to safety, the major concern became the whereabouts of Hausser. What had become of the commander of Seventh Army? The last person to have seen him was Meindl. Was Hausser a prisoner or had he fallen victim to Allied fire? On that fateful day of August 20, just as those SS troops that had escaped death were making preparations for the mounting of a rescue mission, a loud cheer arose as a lone tank appeared out of the smoke and fire blanketing the escape corridor. Lying on top of the tank, part of his face shot away, was Paul Hausser.

Although most of their equipment had been left behind, over a third of the Seventh Army had managed to elude capture and escape from the pocket in order to fight again. Faced with certain disaster thanks to the Mortain Offensive, the German troops had struggled valiantly to stave off total annihilation. That the bill was not higher is in no small measure attributable to Hausser's skillful maneuvering of his units. As a further indication of the reverence that Hausser was held in; the SS troops that had escaped from the hell of the pocket were prepared to re-enter in order to save their commander.

A long period of recuperation now followed for Hausser as conditions in the West continued to deteriorate. Seventh Army was reconstituted and continued to bitterly contest the Allied advance with many of those formations that had escaped Falaise. Hausser's loyal II SS Panzer Corps was pulled out for refit and sent to a quiet town in Holland by the name of Arnhem. There they were once more to offer a nasty surprise for Montgomery.

After a lengthy recuperation, Hausser was once again summoned by Hitler to assume field command. This time he was sent to command Army Group G facing General Patton's advance through the Palatinate. However, by this time the war was irrevocably lost and there was little Hausser could do to alter events. Despite the renowned fanaticism, he refused to practice Hitler's scorched earth policy and by doing so, contributed to Germany's post-war recovery.

How does Hausser measure up to the greatness of other German Generals? Very credibly indeed. After building the Waffen SS he led these formations with skill and success. Hausser was the last German General to launch a successful offensive in the East at Kharkov. At Tarnopol, Kursk and in the Crimea his formations had fought brilliantly and with great success. The reputation of the Waffen SS as very formidable fighting units stemmed from the success garnered by Hausser's II SS Panzer Corps. As an organizer he proved his skill beyond doubt and as a Corps commander, he had few peers. Strategically, he was untested but his handling of Seventh Army left little room for grand maneuvers and the wound suffered at Falaise prevented him from retaining high command.

Only one option was left to him at Falaise and so his strategic talent went untried. After he became disenchanted with Hitler's demands to hang on at all costs. More and more he acted independently. As for why he launched the Mortain Offensive when he was in total disagreement with the concept, one can only speculate. Perhaps both he and Eberbach, aware that each other were both loyal to the regime, were reluctant to express their feelings lest the other concur with Hitler.

Perhaps the most formidable block to Hausser's receiving the credit due him is the stigma attached to him by his association with the dreaded SS. Immediately after the war attention was called to the atrocities committed by a few SS formations during their withdrawal through France. Then too, the headlines denouncing the Malmedy massacre made association with the SS an athema to victors anxious to seek retribution. Hausser's record as a Corps commander, was matched by few during the entire war and he justly deserves recognition as a talented and very capable General.

At Nuremberg, Hausser steadfastly clung to his opinion that the Waffen SS was no different than any other fighting force and deserved treatment as such. Although the SS as a unit was placed on trial, Hausser never wavered in his convictions.

After the war, Hausser published the first comprehensive history of the Waffen SS. Though naturally shaded to show the SS in a favorable light, it was nonetheless a remarkable chronicle.

Hausser continued his efforts to vindicate the Waffen SS during the post-war years. He contended that just like any other army, it had its share of misfits and sadists. Regular army discipline usually manages to keep fanaticism in check but because Nazi Germany was a police state dominated by other branches of the SS, the criminal element in the Waffen SS formations were allowed to proceed with little fear of punishment. Hitler's low opinion of his generals was no secret and few were the commanders who were ready to insist that appropriate punishment be meted out to the SS criminals. Consequently, enough atrocities were carried out to forever blemish the fighting record of the Waffen SS. Therefore, Hausser was guilty of 'guilt by association' and has been denied the credit due him as field commander.

During the decade of the fifties, two illustrious German Generals sprang to the defense of the Waffen SS. The last chief of the General Staff, Heinz Guderian wrote:

"Our honor is our loyalty." This was the motto according to which the Waffen SS was trained, and it was the motto according to which it fought. Whoever saw them in battle is bound to confirm that. After the collapse this formation faced exceptionally heavy and unjust charges . . . Since so many untrue and unjust things have been said and written about them, I welcome most cordially the initiative of their prewar teacher and one of the most outstanding wartime commanders, who has taken up his pen to give evidence of the truth. His book will help to disperse the clouds of lies and calumnies piled up around the Waffen SS and will help those gallant men to resume the place they deserve alongside the other branches of the Wehrmacht."[10]

Colonel General Hasso von Maunteuffel, a much respected and admired Panzer General, while serving as a member of the West German Government, took up the fight on behalf of the Waffen SS. Finally, the Bundestag voted to grant the veterans of the Waffen SS equal status to the Wehrmacht. Hausser had won his final victory.

To those close to the war, the Waffen SS was a symbol of an elite and fanatical organization of fighting men. Paul Hausser was the single largest contributor to the success and construction of this unit. After molding it in the image he desired, he led it on the field of battle with brilliance and dignity. Although other SS Generals such as Steiner and Meyer proved their worth in battle, there can be little doubt that Hausser's military talent overshadowed all others. After a truly remarkable career as trainer, soldier, organizer, and spokesman, Paul Hausser died at the age of 92 in 1972, respected by his former SS comrades-in-arms and Wehrmacht veterans alike.

Notes

Introduction

1. Colonel Trevor N. Dupuy, *A Genius for War*, p. 48.

Chapter 1 Notes

1. Heinz Guderian, *Panzer Leader*, pp. 10.
2. Kenneth Macksey, *Guderian, Creator of the Blitzkrieg*, pp. 101.
3. Guderian, *op cit.* pp. 80.
4. *Ibid*, pp. 85.
5. *Ibid*, pp. 88.
6. David Downing, *The Devil's Virtuosos*, pp. 110.
7. Telford Taylor, *The March of Conquest*.
8. Guderian, *op cit.* pp. 84.
9. *Ibid*, pp. 97–98.
10. Michael Carver ed., *The War Lords* pp. 309.
11. *Ibid*, pp. 313.

Chapter 2 Notes

1. John Keegan, *Rundstedt*, p. 25.
2. *Ibid*, p. 66.
3. Erich von Manstein, *Lost Victories*, p. 23.
4. Keegan, *op cit.*, p. 78.
5. *Ibid*, p. 80.
6. *Ibid*, p. 110.
7. *Ibid*, p. 144.
8. *Ibid*, p. 159.

Chapter 3 Notes

1. Scoullar, J. L., *Battle for Egypt*, pp. 372–373.
2. Churchill, Winston, *The Grand Alliance*, p. 660.
3. Cave-Brown, Anthony, *Bodyguard of Lies*, pp. 96–97.

Chapter 4 Notes

1. Von Manstein, Fritz Erich, *Lost Victories*, pp. 202–03.
2. Carell, Paul, *Hitler Moves East*, p. 579.
3. Von Manstein, *op cit.*, p. 304.
4. *Ibid*, p. 389.
5. Ziemke, Earl F., *Stalingrad to Berlin, the German Defeat in the East*, p. 87.
6. Carell, Paul, *Scorched Earth*, p. 175.
7. *Ibid*, p. 178.
8. *Ibid*, p. 183.
9. *Ibid*, p. 186.
10. *Ibid*, p. 194.
11. Downing, David, *The Devil's Virtuosos*, p. 135.
12. Von Manstein, *op cit.*, p. 544.
13. Von Manstein, op cit., p. 544.

Chapter 5 Notes

1. Kenneth Macksey, *Kesselring: The Making of the Luftwaffe*, p. 15.
2. *Ibid*, p. 28.
3. Jacques Benoist-Mechin, *60 Days That Shook the West*, p. 89.
4. Albert Kesselring, *Kesselring, A Soldier's Record*, p. 72.
5. *Ibid*, p. 97.
6. *Ibid*, p. 110.
7. *Ibid*, p. 107.
8. *Ibid*, p. 141.
9. Macksey, *op. cit.*, p. 113.
10. Kesselring, *op. cit.*, p. 176.
11. *Ibid*, p. 199.
12. *Ibid*, p. 210.

13. Macksey, *op. cit.*, p. 176.
14. Kesselring, *op. cit.*, p. 224.
15. *Ibid*, p. 225.
16. Martin Blumenson, *Salerno to Cassino*, p. 143.
17. Macksey, *op. cit.*, p. 192.
18. Blumenson, *op. cit.*, pp. 311–312.
19. Macksey, *op. cit.*, p. 210.
20. Kesselring, *op. cit.*, p. 234.
21. *Ibid*, p. 250.
22. Macksey, *op. cit.*, p. 219.
23. *Ibid*, p. 224.
24. Kesselring, *op. cit.*, p. 265.
25. *Ibid*, p. 305.
26. *Ibid*, p. 328.
27. *Ibid*, p. 331.

Chapter 6 Notes

1. Heinz Hohne, *The Order of the Death's Head*, p. 442.
2. Paul Carell, *Scorched Earth*, p. 179.
3. *Ibid*, p. 181.
4. Martin Caidin, *The Tigers are Burning*, p. 90.
5. Major General F.W. von Mellenthin, *Panzer Battles*, p. 219.
6. Martin Caidin, *The Tigers are Burning*, p. 189.
7. Major General F. W. von Mellenthin, *Panzer Battles*, p. 281.
8. Martin Caidin, *The Tigers are Burning*, p. 218.
9. Eddy Florentin, *The Battle of the Falaise Gap*, p. 258.
10. George Stein, *The Waffen SS*, p. 254.

Bibliography

Introduction

1. Dupuy, Col. Trevor N. *A Genius for War, the German Army and General Staff 1807-1945*, A T.N. Dupuy Associates Book, Dun Loring 1977.
2. Goerlitz, Walter. *History of the German General Staff*, Praeger, New York 1977.
3. Leach, Barry. *German General Staff*, Ballantine Books, New York 1973.

Chapter 1 Bibliography

Beaufre, Andre, *1940, The Fall of France*, Alfred Knopf, New York 1968.

Bethel, Nicholas, *The War Hitler Won*, Holt, Rinehart & Winston, New York 1972.

Carver, Michael, Ed., *The War Lords*, Little Brown & Co., Boston 1976.

Chapman, Guy, *Why France Fell*, Holt, Rinehart & Winston, New York 1968.

Downing, David, *The Devil's Virtuosos*, St. Martin's Press, New York 1977.

Guderian, Heinz, *Panzer Leader*, E.P. Dutton, New York 1952.

Horne, Alistair, *To Lose A Battle*, Little Brown & Co., Boston 1969.

Keegan, John, *Guderian*, Ballantine Books, New York 1973.

Keegan, John, *Barbarossa, The Invasion Of Russia 1941*, Ballantine Books, New York 1971.

Macksey, Kenneth, *Guderian, Creator Of The Blitzkrieg*, Stein & Day, New York 1976.

Benoist-Mechin, Jacques, *60 Days That Shook The West*, G. P. Putnam & Sons, New York 1963.

Williams, John, *The Ides Of May*. Alfred Knopf, New York 1968.

Young, Peter, Ed., *Atlas Of The Second World War* G.P. Putnam & Sons, New York 1974.

Chapter 2 Bibliography

Baldwin, Hanson, *The Crucial Years 1939–1941*, Harper & Row Publishers, N.Y. 1976.

Bethel, Nicholas, *The War Hitler Won*, Holt, Rinehart and Winston, New York 1972.

Carver, Field Marshal Sir Michael, *The War Lords*, Little Brown & Co., Boston, 1976.

Cave-Brown, Anthony, *Bodyguard of Lies*, Harper & Row Publishers, N.Y. 1975.

Downing, David, *The Devil's Virtuosos*, St. Martin's Press, N.Y. 1977.

Irving, David, *The Trail of the Fox*, Dutton, N.Y. 1977.

Keegan, John, *Rundstedt*, Ballantine Books, N.Y. 1974.

Lewin, Ronald, *Ultra Goes to War*, McGraw-Hill, N.Y. 1978.

Liddell-Hart, B. H., *History of the Second World War*, G. P. Putnam Sons, N.Y. 1970.

Manstein, Field Marshal Erich von, *Lost Victories*, Henry Regnery Co., N.Y. 1958.

Macksey, Kenneth, *Guderian, Creator of the Blitzkrieg*, Stein and Day, N.Y. 1975.

Merriam, Robert E., *Dark December*, Ziff Davis Publishing Co., 1947.

Chapter 3 Bibliography

Barnett, Corelli, *The Desert Generals*, Viking Press, New York 1961.

Blumenson, Martin, *Kasserine Pass*, Houghton Mifflin Co., Boston 1967.

Carell, Paul, *The Foxes Of The Desert*, E. P. Dutton & Co., New York 1961.

Cave-Brown, Anthony, *Bodyguard of Lies*, Harper & Row, New York 1975.

Churchill, Winston, *The Second World War, The Grand Alliance*, Houghton Mifflin Co., Boston 1950.

Douglas-Home, Charles, *Rommel*, Saturday Review Press, New York 1973.

Hamilton, J.A.I. and Turner, L.C.F., *Sidi-Rezegh Battles*, Oxford University Press, London 1957.

Holmes, Richard, *Bir Hakim*, Ballantine Books, New York 1971.

Irving, David, *The Trail Of The Fox*, Thomas Congdon Books, New York 1977.

Jablonski, David, *The Desert Warriors*, Lancer Books, New York 1972.

Jackson, W.G.F., *The Battle For North Africa*, Mason/ Charter, New York 1975.

Liddell-Hart, Basil, *The Rommel Papers*, Harcourt Brace & Co., New York 1953.

Lewin, Ronald, *Rommel As Military Commander*, B. T. Batsford Ltd, London 1968.

Lewin, Ronald, *Ultra Goes To War*, Hill Book Co., New York 1978.

Macksey, Kenneth, *Afrika Korps*, Ballantine Books, New York 1968.

Orpen, Neil, *War In The Desert, Vol III*, Purnell, London.

Playfair, I.S.O. et al, *The Mediterranean And Middle East Vol III*, Her Majesty's Stationary Office, London 1960.

Rutherford, Ward, *Kasserine, Baptism Of Fire*, Ballantine Books, New York 1970.

Scmidt, H. W., *With Rommel In The Desert*, Ballantine Books, New York 1951.

Scoullar, J.L., *Battle For Egypt*, War History Branch. New Zealand in the Second World War. Geoffrey Cumberlege, Oxford University Press, London 1955.

Strawson, John, *The Battle For North Africa*, Charles Scribner's Sons, New York 1969.

Tute, Warren, *The North African War*, Sedgwick & Jackson, 1976.

Von Mellenthin, F. W., *Panzer Battles*, University of Oklahoma Press, Norman 1956.

Warlimont, Walter, *Inside Hitler's Headquarters 1939-1945 Frederick A. Prager, New York 1964.*

Winterbotham, F. W., The Ultra Secret, Harper & Row, New York 1974.

Young, Desmond, *Rommel, The Desert Fox*, Harper & Row, New York 1950

Chapter 4 Bibliography

Carell, Paul, H., *Hitler Moves East 1941-1943*, Little Brown and Co., Boston 1963.

Carell, Paul, *Scorched Earth*, Little Brown and Co., Boston 1966.

Carver, Michael, *The War Lords*, Little Brown and Co., Boston 1976.

Caidin, Martin, *The Tigers Are Burning*, Hawthorn Publishers, New York 1974.

Clark, Alan, *Barbarossa*, William Morrow and Company, New York 1965.

Goerlitz, Walter, *Paulus and Stalingrad*, Greenwood Press, 1960 reprinted 1974.

Kerr, Walter, *The Secret of Stalingrad*, Doubleday and Co. Inc., New York 1978.

Liddell-Hart, B. H., *History Of The Second World War*, G. P. Putnam's Sons, New York 1970.

Von Manstein, Fritz Erich von, *Lost Victories*, Henry Regnery Co., New York 1958.

Seaton, Albert, *The Russo-German War 1941-45*, Praeger Publishers, New York 1971.

Seaton, Albert, *Stalin As Military Commander*, Praeger Publishers, New York 1975.

Ziemke, Earl F., *Stalingrad To Berlin: The German Defeat In The East*, Office of the Chief of Military History, Washington D.C., 1968.

Chapter 5 Bibliography

Adelman, Robert H. & Walton, Col. George, *Rome Fall Today*, Little Brown & Co., Boston 1968.

Benoist-Mechin, Jacques, *Sixty Days That Shook the West*, G. P. Putnams & Sons, New York 1963.

Blumensen, Martin, *Anzio: The Gamble That Failed*, J. P. Lippincott Co., New York 1963.

Blumenson, Martin, *Bloody River*, Houghton Mifflin Co., Boston 1970.

Blumenson, Martin, *Salerno To Cassino*, Office of the Chief of Military History, Wash., D.C. 1969.

Fisher Jr. Ernest F., *Cassino To The Alps*, Office of the Chief of Military History, Wash., D.C. 1977.

Jackson, W.G.F., *The Battle For Italy*, Harper and Row, New York 1967.

Kesselring, Albert, *Kesselring, A Soldier's Record*, Greenwood Press—Reprint, New York 1970.

Kurzman, Dan, *The Race For Rome*, Doubleday &Co. Inc., New York 1975.

Lewin, Ronald, *Ultra Goes To War*, McGraw Hill, New York 1978.

Macksey, Kenneth, *Kesselring, The Making of the Luftwaffe*, David McKay Co. Inc., New York 1978.

Orgill, Douglas, *The Gothic Line*, Library Editions Publishing Co., New York 1967.

Smith, E.D., *The Battles For Cassino*, Charles Scribner's Sons, New York 1975.

Whiting, Charles, *The End of the War*, Stein and Day, New York 1973.

Winterbotham, F.W., *The Ultra Secret*, Harper and Row, New York 1974.

Chapter 6 *Bibliography*

Barker, James & Lucas, James, *The Battle of Normandy, The Falaise Gap*, Holmes & Meier, New York, 1978.

Bennett, Ralph, *Ultra in the West*, Charles Scribners Sons, New York, 1980.

Butler, Rupert, *The Black Angels*, St. Martins Press, New York, 1979.

Caidin, Martin, *The Tigers are Burning*, Hawthorn Books, New York, 1974.

Carell, Paul, *Hitler Moves East*, Little Brown & Co., Boston, 1964.

Carell, Paul, *Scorched Earth*, Little Brown &Co., Boston, 1970.

Clark, Alan, *Barbarossa*, Willian Morrow & Co., New York, 1965.

Dowding, David, *The Devil's Virtuosos*, St. Martins Press, New York, 1977.

Florentin, Eddy, *The Battle of the Falaise Gap*, Hawthorn Books, New York, 1967.

Graber, G.S., *The History of the S.S.*, David McKay, New York, 1978.

Grunberger, Richard, *Hitler's S.S.*, Delacorte Press, New York, 1970.

Guderian, Heinz, *Panzer Leader*, E.P. Dutton & Co., New York, 1952.

Hohne, Heinz, *The Order of the Death's Head*, Coward McCann, New York, 1970.

Keegan, John, *Waffen S.S.*, Ballantine Books, New York, 1970.

Lucas, James, *Germany's Elite Panzer Force—Grossdeutschland*, MacDonald & James, London, 1978.

Manstein, Field Marshal Erich von, *Lost Victories*, Henry Regnery Co., New York, 1968.

Mellenthin, General F.W. von, *Panzer Battles*, Oklahoma University, Norman, 1956.

Seaton, Albert, *The Russo-German War*, Praeger, New York, 1971.

Stein, George, *The Waffen S.S. 1939–1945*, Cornell University, Ithaca, 1966.

Taylor, Telford, *The March of Conquest*, Simon & Shuster, New York, 1958.

Wilmot, Chester, *The Struggle for Europe*, Harper & Row, New York, 1952.

Wykes, Alan, *Hitler's Bodyguards*, Ballantine Books, New York, 1974.

Ziemke, Earl F., *Stalingrad to Berlin*, Government Printing Office, Washington, D.C., 1968.

A TERRIFYING OCCULT TRILOGY
by William W. Johnstone

THE DEVIL'S KISS   (1498, $3.50)
As night falls on the small prairie town of Whitfield, red-rimmed eyes look out from tightly shut windows. An occasional snarl rips from once-human throats. Shadows play on dimly lit streets, bringing with the darkness an almost tangible aura of fear. For the time is now right in Whitfield. The beasts are hungry, and the Undead are awake . . .

THE DEVIL'S HEART   (1526, $3.50)
It was the summer of 1958 that the horror surfaced in the town of Whitfield. Those who survived the terror remember it as the summer of The Digging—the time when Satan's creatures rose from the bowels of the earth and the hot wind began to blow. The town is peaceful, and the few who had fought against the Prince of Darkness before believed it could never happen again.

THE DEVIL'S TOUCH   (1491, $3.50)
The evil that triumphed during the long-ago summer in Whitfield still festers in the unsuspecting town of Logandale. Only Sam and Nydia Balon, lone survivors of the ancient horror, know the signs—the putrid stench rising from the bowels of the earth, the unspeakable atrocities that mark the foul presence of the Prince of Darkness. Hollow-eyed, hungry corpses will rise from unearthly tombs to engorge themselves on living flesh and spawn a new generation of restless Undead . . . and only Sam and Nydia know what must be done.

Available wherever paperbacks are sold, or order direct from the Publisher. Send cover price plus 50¢ per copy for mailing and handling to Zebra Books, Dept. 1752, 475 Park Avenue South, New York, N.Y. 10016. DO NOT SEND CASH.